For my mother, Hilly Davies

CURRENT ISSUES IN BUSINESS ETHICS

Edited by Peter W.F. Davies

London and New York

First published 1997
by Routledge
11 New Fetter Lane, London EC4P 4EE

Simultaneously published in the USA and Canada
by Routledge
29 West 35th Street, New York, NY 10001

© 1997 selection and editorial matter, Peter W. F. Davies;
individual chapters, the contributors

Typeset in Times by Routledge
Printed and bound in Great Britain by Redwood Books,
Trowbridge, Wiltshire

British Library Cataloguing in Publication Data
A catalogue record for this book is available from the British Library

Library of Congress Cataloguing in Publication Data
A catalogue record for this book has been requested

ISBN 0–415–12449–2 (hbk)
ISBN 0–415–12450–6 (pbk)

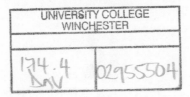

CONTENTS

CONTENTS

CONTRIBUTORS

William A. Bain is a part-time lecturer and PhD candidate at The Management School, Imperial College, London. His thesis investigates the corporate culture and defensive behaviour that underlie safety management in a multinational oil company. The research, 'which is finally nearing completion', is based on an ethnographic study carried out in four countries. William has an MBA from the Rotterdam School of Management/Erasmus University, and an engineering degree from Queen's University, Canada. He has worked in industry as a construction supervisor, operations engineer and organisational behaviour advisor. In an effort to broaden their cultural horizons, William and family have recently relocated to Singapore.

Jim Barry is a political sociologist and teaches in Organisation Studies. He spent many years studying part-time (at North-East London Polytechnic and Birkbeck College) while working as an administrator in London's local government. He joined the University of East London in 1987 and is currently Co-director of the University's *Organisation Studies Research Group*. He is involved in two long-term research projects: one into gender and urban governance in London and Mumbai (formerly Bombay); another into gender and organisations with particular reference to Higher education.

Stephen Brigley has taught, researched and published on management and professional ethics at universities and colleges in the UK (following posts in teaching and teacher training in the 1980s). His interests and publications also include school management, governance and accountability (doctoral thesis), moral and social education, and research methodology. Since March 1995 he has been the Education, Research and Development Officer at the Faculty of Public Health Medicine, Royal College of Physicians.

Raff Carmen   is a lecturer in Adult Education, Adult Literacy, and Rural Social and Community Development at the Centre for Adult and Higher Education (CAHE) at Manchester University. He is on the editorial board of *Development*, the Journal of SID (Rome), and a member of the DSA Development Ethics Group (UK). He is author of *Autonomous Development: The Humanisation of the Landscape*, and *Communication, Education and Empowerment*. He also contributed to Harcourt (ed.) *Feminist Perspectives on Sustainable Development*.

Heather Clark   is a sociologist who spent a number of years working in industry before entering education, where she taught a wide variety of courses. She currently teaches in Organisation Studies and is involved in a long-term research project into gender and organisations with particular reference to Higher Education. In addition to coordinating Business Studies at Queen Mary and Westfield College, she is Co-director of the University of East London's Organisation Studies Research Group.

Peter W. F. Davies   is currently senior lecturer in Strategic Management and Business Ethics at Buckinghamshire College (a College of Brunel University). He teaches both subjects on under- and postgraduate courses. He was a founder member of COPE (The Centre for Organisational and Professional Ethics) with colleagues at Brunel University. Formerly a mining and production engineer, he is now developing research in engineering ethics. His PhD thesis was entitled 'The Contribution of the Philosophy of Technology to the Management of Technology'.

Patrick Flood   (PhD, London School of Economics) is Associate Professor of Human Resource Management at the Department of Personnel and Employment Relations, University of Limerick, Ireland. Former British Council Scholar at LSE, and Fulbright Scholar at the University of Maryland at College Park, he has authored three books, including *Managing without Traditional Methods* (Addison Wesley, 1995). During 1994–96 he was the EU Post-Doctoral Fellow in Organisational Behaviour at the London

Business School. His research interests include top management teams, resource-based views on human resource strategy, and union organisation.

Marek Lubelski   is currently working on an international Local Agenda 21 project with Bedfordshire County Council and The World Wide Fund for Nature. Before this he coordinated Open Ground – a North London community-based environment/education initiative, which supports the design of sustainable communities and business. He has taught in Adult, Further and Higher Education, and co-authored a number of papers on sustainability.

Iain Munro   is a Teaching and Research Fellow at the Warwick Business School. His current research interests revolve around the idea of ethics for the management sciences, with particular reference to the areas of Information Systems and Operational Research. Previous to his position at Warwick he was a doctoral student at the University of Hull. His work is partly funded by the ESRC.

Angela Peek   is a PhD researcher at the International Management Research Centre, Buckinghamshire College (a College of Brunel University). She is currently researching into ethical and cultural difference that arise in Western/Russian joint ventures. She previously carried out research into whistleblowing at Luton University. She is on the national executive of the European Business Ethics Network (UK), and joint editor of the EBEN-UK newsletter. She also edits a number of business information magazines and newsletters, including the *International Tax Review*, and *Croner's Exporter's Briefing*.

Keith Pheby   has been involved in both teaching and research in the area of organisational ethics in America, Great Britain and Japan, where he is currently engaged as Visiting Professor in the Faculty of Economics at Dashisha University, Kyoto. He is particularly interested in the relationship between ethics and power and the possibility of designing corporate structures capable of sustaining ethical cultures. He is also a director of Fractos Ltd, which designs computer-gaming simulations to aid organisations in this process. His publications include *Interventions: Displacing the Metaphysical Subject*, Washington DC, 1988.

Jane Pritchard   graduated in Philosophy and Literature from Warwick University in 1974 and afterwards qualified and practised as a solicitor in both the private and public sectors. From August 1993 she was a Research Assistant at the Centre for Professional Ethics, which is part of the University of Central Lancashire in Preston. She was working on the Centre's project on professional codes of conduct.

Philip Stiles   is a Research Fellow in Organisational Behaviour at London Business School. He has worked on major projects in corporate governance, strategic human resource management, and organisational ethics. Before joining LBS, he was a Research Fellow at Henley Management College. Philip is executive editor of the international strategy journal *Long Range Planning*, and is the author of numerous articles.

Peter Vass   is Research Director of the Centre for the Study of Regulated Industries (CRI) and a senior lecturer in accounting and finance at the School of Management, University of Bath. He started his career as an economist in the Government Economic Service and worked in the Departments of Transport and Environment. He then qualified as an accountant. He was head of Technical and Research at the Chartered Institute of Public Finance and Accountancy until 1990. The CRI was established in March 1991, and publishes research reports, discussion papers and proceedings, and industry statistics.

Simon Webley   has been director of the British–North American Research Association (BNARA) since 1969. He read economics at Trinity College, Dublin, and now directs research on international economics and business behaviour issues. He is a Senior Visiting Fellow at the City University Business School and consultant to the Institute of Business Ethics (IBE). His recent publications include *Continuing Education and Training of the Workforce*, 1992 (with Professor Sir Frederick Crawford), and *Applying Codes of Business Ethics: A Report on Best Practice*, 1995.

Andrew Wilson   is Associate Director of the Ashbridge Research Centre for Business and Society. The focus of the Centre is an investigation into the rapidly changing relationship between public, private and voluntary sector organisations. Within this theme, the

Centre conducts research into two inter-related issues: the relation-ship between corporate competitiveness and accountability to stake-holders; and the role of business as stakeholder in society. Andrew is the author and co-author of several reports, including *The Importance of Being Ethical, Corporate Giving*, and a forthcoming report for the Joseph Rowntree foundation on cross-sectoral part-nership management. He is co-tutor on the joint Ashbridge/ Business in the Community four-day development programme, *Managing Corporate Community Involvement*.

ACKNOWLEDGEMENTS

I think it is probably impossible to complete this page in an ethical and just manner, because of the difficulty in truly ascertaining who precisely has helped, in which way, during the long course of producing this book; some people are bound not to be given due credit, their contribution lost in the mists of time – and the longer the list, the worse it gets. However, it *is* ethical to do the best one can in an imperfect world, so here goes.

My thanks first of all to Ruth Chadwick and Andrew Belsey, the editors of the *Routledge Series in Professional Ethics*, who took a risk in first asking me to put this book together. Thanks also to Richard Stoneman at Routledge for his patience and flexibility concerning deadlines. This book also of course has fifteen other contributors besides myself, and they have been very good not only in contributing their chapters, but also in digging out detailed information to satisfy my pernickety nature for attention to detail when it comes to referencing sources.

Next, some names which will mean nothing to the reader, but who have been a source of personal encouragement and who have helped me keep life, and writing, in perspective; Bronwyn Armstrong, Sara Gibbons, Bob Redfern, Angela Thorburn and Gavin Whitton.

Finally, thanks to my children Yolanda and Samuel, who continually remind me what is important in life.

INTRODUCTION

There has been a fair deluge of UK books on business ethics in recent years, so it seems reasonable first of all to explain why another text on the subject has value. First, the increase in business ethics publications is in *percentage* terms; the actual number of specifically UK texts remains small in number. Second, there remain also some gaps. Ethics are to a significant extent shaped by a country's history and culture (and closely related to its laws), and this lends validity to country-specific texts. This is not to say they have to be inward looking or isolated from global events, merely to point out that such events will be interpreted in a particular way, and both students and business people will benefit from an understanding of business ethics based in the 'home' context. To my knowledge at the time of writing, this is the first UK authored book with new contributions being specifically written for each chapter, structured overall around a pre-determined and logical theme. (Moreover, this is also one of the texts in the *Routledge Series in Professional Ethics*, which has already addressed ethical issues in journalism, nursing and social work; to leave out business would be hard to justify.) Although the contributors are mainly academics, this book essentially sets out to give any reader an accessible introduction into the emerging field of business ethics.

The content has a logical flow from beginning to end (as explained in the following pages), but a reader may choose a particular chapter which covers their field of interest, and then follow it up as guided by the section on *Further Reading* at the end of the book. The book is split into three parts, with the chapters of the final part being longer and more exploratory.

This overall introduction gives a short summary of all the chapters in the book, giving the reader a quick overview of the content,

1

and then explaining the logic of that content. The three parts then each have their own introductions, which summarise and assess the contributions in greater depth. It is recommended that these introductions are read first, before going on to the chapters in each part.

The activity of 'doing business' has had a bad press for a long, long time. Aristotle (384–322 BC) relegated 'making money', along with 'making artifacts', to the same second-order category, *poiesis* (merely a means to an end), whereas the *true* end of human endeavour was considered to be *praxis* – engaging in sport, philosophy and politics. One could argue that the more recent bad press, in the fallout from the grab-it-all 1980s, still follows the same line – business is a somewhat dubious and murky activity, but a necessary means in order to enjoy the 'higher' things in life. Moreover, the business world has provided plenty of negative ammunition for itself in the form of the scandals surrounding Guinness, Maxwell, BCCI, NatWest/Blue Arrow and Lloyds, along with the British Airways/Virgin Atlantic 'dirty tricks' campaign, plus the burning of Piper Alpha, the Clapham rail and the M1 in Leicestershire plane crashes, and the sinkings of the *Marchioness* and the *Herald of Free Enterprise*.

But even without such self-inflicted bad publicity, business organisations, because of their increasing power and pervasiveness, would naturally draw to themselves questions about the responsibility and accountability with which they exercise their power. History shows us that, in times of change, people are reluctant to let go of the 'received wisdom' which has served them so well in the past; eventually, however, the momentum of continuing questioning will create a critical mass whereby the received wisdom (or the old paradigm) is eventually displaced in favour of a new way of looking at things. This book, then, is part of that questioning process, and is an attempt to articulate and draw together some of the main concerns as the public continues to put business under the microscope.

PART I – MACRO ISSUES: THE ROLE AND LEGITIMACY OF BUSINESS ACTIVITY

It would seem that the appropriate place to start a book entitled *Current Issues in Business Ethics* is to examine the nature, meaning and role of business activity itself, and its overall legitimacy in the first place. Many business ethics issues become problems due to the differing understandings of the relevant parties as to what the purpose and meaning of business is.

In Chapter 1, **Peter Davies** outlines five perspectives on this question, some of which are explored in greater depth in later chapters. In common is the recognition that business (maybe by default, and not consciously so) has become a powerful and pervasive force of social and environmental change. Business's continued legitimacy (or 'licence to operate') depends on a public assessment of how it acquits itself, especially in the continuing culture of deregulation. The differing views on business's essential meaning and purpose within wider society are not necessarily mutually exclusive, but can quickly become severely dysfunctional in a fast-changing society.

It certainly seems fair to say that the impact of business on the environment has been a key issue for the last twenty years, and one which has contributed to putting business ethics on the map. In Chapter 2, **Raff Carmen** and **Marek Lubelski** argue the case for the *primary* legitimacy of business being assessed in terms of its track record in delivering genuine sustainable development, particularly since the 1992 Rio Earth Summit and the signing up of 120-plus countries to Agenda 21. Acknowledging that the top-down approach is likely to have little effect, they point towards a groundswell of smaller-scale, regionally based ways of exchanging goods and services, as being more likely to provide the route for genuine change and sustainability.

Developing the theme of legitimacy at the corporate level, **Philip Stiles** focuses in Chapter 3 on Corporate Governance. The changing balance of self-regulation v. legislation, the Cadbury Report, and the ongoing abuses of corporate power reported in the news, all contribute to the governance issue being of continuing concern. What role should shareholders have in controlling a business? What are the obligations to broader society? How can the policing role of non-executive directors be made workable? The answers to such questions all speak volumes to the public about the perceived role of business.

In Chapter 4, **Andrew Wilson** uses the notion of a 'licence to operate' in a changing and more ethically aware external environment to explore business's legitimacy. Consumers, job-seekers, investors and employees are all becoming more discerning. Will this lead in the long run to only the more ethical companies surviving and retaining their licences to operate? Andrew Wilson argues that such is the case – good ethics will eventually prove to be good business.

The notion of the 'stakeholder' model of business is implicit in each of these four chapters, and there will always be a debate about how much emphasis should be put on which stakeholders. Should the wider ecology be the number one concern, displacing shareholders? Should the few be sacrificed for the majority? Deeper in the background of these chapters is the question of legitimacy in terms of *ownership*. Why should those who work in a business mainly have no ownership, working throughout their lives to increase the ROC (return on capital) of anonymous shareholders and investment houses? Perhaps this ownership question is behind a deep-seated unease about accepting the capitalist system of ownership and control? For individuals working in companies, it may manifest itself in the search for meaning *inside* that workplace which takes up such a huge amount of the time and energy of their lives; or indeed in the search for meaning *outside* the workplace. Either way, and for other reasons, there is always a tension between the individual and the organisation of which they are a part. With the questioning about whether it is legitimate for individual managers to give orders to others, and the decline of God as the ultimate workplace supervisor, business organisations are forever seeking ways to motivate people to work, and ways to deal with the inevitable (and often healthy) tensions between the individual and the organisation. A number of angles on this theme are explored in Part II.

PART II – MICRO ISSUES: THE RELATIONSHIP BETWEEN THE INDIVIDUAL AND THE BUSINESS ORGANISATION

The arguments at the *macro* level are important in terms of setting the deep legal, moral and fiscal structure of the places in which people work. But it is at the *micro* level that individuals feel most acutely any ethical dilemma – 'the individual' v. 'the system' (or 'the organisation'). We walk through that office door or factory gate and are somehow immediately aware that we are expected to wear a different ethical hat for the day or the shift. We lay aside our citizens' right to hold our own opinions and be treated as equals, and enter an arena ('the organisation') where we are expected to keep our mouths shut and do without question what our superiors tell us. If we don't like it we have the option of voting with our feet. A somewhat negative and extreme picture, you might say, but from school playground peer-group pressure onwards, we have all surely experienced the power of groups and organisations to make us behave in ways we do not wish to, in ways that in some measure go against our conscience or 'better judgement'. At the very least, the organisation's own 'code' tends quite easily to overrule our own.

It is because of the experiential and asymmetrical power of the (business) organisation, in relation to the ethical behaviour of the individual, that Part II begins in Chapter 5 with **Simon Webley** examining some of its implications. This power of business organisations may have been acquired to some extent by default (i.e. as a result of the decline of the church and the family as centres of meaning and moral guidance). However, its mere existence puts a responsibility on business to be morally 'self aware', whether it likes it or not. Surveys suggest that a very high percentage of managers experience moral dilemmas, but whose ethics should they follow – the company's or their own?

One way of answering this question is through the interesting notion of *ethico-power*, which is introduced by **Keith Pheby** in Chapter 6, and which ties together ethics with that other buzzword, 'empowerment'. Every organisation consists of multiple realities; it is not simply 'the organisation' v. 'the individual'. Power is not a zero-sum game, but can be increased overall given greater trust and sharing of information. In this way a new psychological contract can be developed which enables to actually happen the creativity that organisations say they want.

In Chapter 7, **Jane Pritchard** explores another means frequently advanced to help organisations and individuals live with each other more smoothly – the idea of professionalism; surely this is something both commonly desirable and understood? She argues, though, that trying to get business to be more 'professional', and trying to get the traditional professions (such as medicine and the law) to be more 'businesslike', is counter-productive. Business, if it wants to be more ethical, must change its ways within its own value-system; it can go no further than merely pretend to be professional because its essential motives are different.

In Chapter 8, **Iain Munro** examines the role of the Code of Ethics as a means to help people and organisations live with each other. He points out their benefits and limitations, and identifies as key the process of drawing up the codes in the first place, and then enforcing them. Codes can clear some of the grey areas, but they do not solve individual dilemmas nor do they address underlying structural and cultural issues (often the causes of ethical problems). Codes can also be used, however, as springboards to raise the climate of ethical debate within an organisation, and hence contribute to tackling some of the underlying issues.

Finally in this part, **Angela Peek** in Chapter 9 looks at whistle-blowing, one of the most visible outcomes of not dealing adequately with the ethical dimension of individual–organisation relationships. Issues of confidentiality and loyalty are at the heart here, as well as those of moral and professional autonomy. The law is currently inadequate[1] and whistleblowing *may* be a legitimate last resort when all other avenues have been exhausted, but it is the least desirable route for all parties concerned. Hence organisations need a number of alternative avenues and mechanisms to deal with ethical issues. A 'whistleblowers' checklist' is also included.

It seems that the larger macro-social changes in expectations discussed in Part I are leading to increasingly difficult situations at the micro-organisational level, as discussed in Part II. Business has found itself trying to fulfil the role of being a surrogate family, providing emotional support, and at the same time being a surrogate church, delivering remedial moral teaching. The latter it does through its Codes of Ethics and various calls for employees to 'act more "professionally"', but simultaneously it comes down extremely hard on potential or actual whistleblowers, who, one assumes, are trying to act 'professionally', often by trying to uphold their professional or company code. *A conflicting message is therefore being sent out.* Similarly, organisations talk of empowerment and want creative diversity, but then constrict their employees by being stuck in the old mentality of bureaucratic rationality which leads to 'power over' rather than to genuine empowerment.

It is in this last respect that Keith Pheby's chapter makes a valuable contribution with his notion of ethico-power and the new psychological contract between the individual and the organisation; but how will the idea be made concrete in organisational life? The business world understands well that if it does not regulate itself adequately, and is seen publicly so to do, then eventually a whole raft of new laws will do it anyway and will infringe upon business's much treasured freedoms. This no doubt at least partially explains the growth in company Codes of Ethics, which is obviously one of the more popular ways of trying to institutionalise business ethics while staving off the law. But the world never stands still, and there are some significant longer-term trends which will have an impact on the institutionalisation of business ethics ideas, and business will have to take serious note of them.

PART III – SOME CURRENT TRENDS AND THEIR IMPACT ON BUSINESS ETHICS

The four major trends discussed in Part III each have their own important implications for the future institutionalisation of Business Ethics. The topics selected stem more from socio-political trends, which, it could be argued, are becoming increasingly cultur- ally embedded in our society, and therefore business, and business ethics, will have to come to terms with them.

In Chapter 10, **Bill Bain** looks at the implications of one of the defining characteristics of the business world in the latter half of the twentieth century, that of globalisation. He does this by focus- ing on the activities of multinational companies (MNCs) operating in less-developed host countries. Here, the question is how to main- tain an ethical balance between respecting local cultures, upholding what are arguably universal ethical norms, and enabling all this to happen within a particular organisational culture. The difficult issue of the global regulation of MNCs is also addressed.

In Chapter 11, **Heather Clark** and **Jim Barry** tackle the neglected area of how trends in the changing gender balance might affect business ethics. They critically evaluate the evidence to suggest that 'women are more ethical than men', and the resulting question that if this is so, will it bring with it more ethical behaviour in business? They tie this in with examining the evidence to suggest that women 'manage' in a different way to men, and that women have to behave more like men in order to be achievers in the current business world. They conclude that the current focus on gender *difference* requires a complementary focus on gender *similarity*, and as such will have to take into account other reasons for behaviour difference, such as social class, age, ethnicity and religion.

In Chapter 12, **Steve Brigley** and **Peter Vass** look at the implica- tions for business ethics of the ongoing trend for privatisation, with particular emphasis on the utilities such as Water, Gas and Rail. They contrast 'private sector ethics' with 'public service ethics', and draw on their own research into how the chairmen of newly privatised utilities understand their role in relation to public *service*. The (in)adequacy of the legal and regulatory framework of the privatised utilities is discussed, and some tentative proposals are suggested to clarify the ethical confusion that utilities' directors experience.

Finally, in Chapter 13, **Patrick Flood** and **Philip Stiles** examine the implications of the decreasing influence of the trade unions in the 1980s and 1990s. They focus on one question: the dangers inherent in an organisational environment where management is unconstrained by union presence. This then leads to suggesting ways in which trade unions can find a *new* role, making a positive contribution in terms of being a regulatory ethical, and economic, mechanism. Evidence that de-unionised firms and industries have lower, and greater, disparity in wages is assessed – as is also the current popular idea that Human Resources Management (HRM) can replace a union's role. They conclude that unions *do* have an important economic and ethical role to play for companies, but this conclusion is set against the background of continuing decline in union membership and the growth of new management techniques which tend to undermine the trade unions' role.

The issues examined in this book are by no means exhaustive but are intended to give the reader an overall appreciation of current issues in the field, issues which are also likely to remain topical for many years. Business is an *activity*, with daily actions and decisions which have far-reaching consequences. Philosophy and ethics help here because it is the purpose of philosophy to consider the nature, purpose and meaning of things, and of ethics in particular to examine the bases for right and authentic *action*. We live in an imperfect and ambiguous world – that much is clear, especially so in business – but to inhabit this imperfect world (and the business world in particular) is an activity that can be done well or badly. As MacIntyre suggests,[2] to do it badly we can either refuse to admit our complicity in the situation, or admit our complicity but state that we can do nothing about it. MacIntyre deems neither course to be satisfactory. I hope this book stimulates the reader to consider 'what ought to be', rather than 'what is currently', accepted in business; if so, then it will have served a valid purpose.

Peter W. F. Davies
Buckinghamshire College (a College of Brunel University)
September, 1996

NOTES

1 At the time of writing (September 1996), the Public Interest Disclosure Bill (formerly named the Whistleblower Protection Bill) is being discussed in Parliament; it has all-party support. See note 8 in Chapter 9.
2 Macintyre, Alasdair (1977) *Why are the Problems of Business Ethics Insoluble?*, conference proceedings from Bentley College, pp. 99–107.

Part I

MACRO ISSUES

The role and legitimacy of business activity

INTRODUCTION TO PART I

Part I – *Macro Issues: The role and legitimacy of business activity* has four contributions. In Chapter 1, *Business Philosophy: Searching for an authentic role*, Peter Davies sets out to get to the heart of various perspectives on the meaning and purpose of business activity in the first place. As is suggested, if we believe the purpose of business is 'to maximise profit', then our viewpoint on business ethics will differ considerably from that of those who believe its purpose is 'to provide meaningful employment'. The five different perspectives Davies discusses point towards business's basic meaning and purpose as a vocation, as a crucial upholder of democracy, as a way of leaving the planet in better shape, as a financial wealth creator, and as a forum for developing people's virtuous characters. Each perspective makes a valid contribution, but in the end the context of time and place will suggest that one may be particularly more relevant and necessary than the others. The question is not so much 'which is the right one?', but 'which perspective (or paradigm) will prevail, and will it prevail at the appropriate time?' Certainly, four of the five perspectives suggest a broadening-out of the values associated with business, but with the current Friedmanite 'business is business' paradigm being long established and well entrenched, it seems that only a major crisis for business survival will actually provide a basis for a genuine challenge to this worldview.

In Chapter 2, *Whose business is it anyway? The question of sustainability*, Marek Lubelski and Raff Carmen put the case that the prevailing emphasis in the 1990s and beyond should be genuine sustainable development; herein lies the true role and legitimacy of business. Of all the external forces pressing on business, it is probably correct to say that the environmental one has been the most strong and persistent. The 1992 Rio Earth Summit got leaders of over 120 nations to sign up to Agenda 21, but is any real change happening? At the senior business level, Lubelski and Carmen suggest not. Despite various promising initiatives and some rigorous investigative research which they outline, the 'business is business' and 'North over South' views still predominate – we continue to have *mal*development. But at a different level they suggest that all is not lost. Cultural resistance to the old paradigm (the culture of competition and power) is manifesting itself at grassroots level in the form of the popular (or informal) economy. These are more regionally based, and provide smaller scale and genuinely sustainable ways of exchanging goods and services. In this they point to the ecosystems perspective, outlined in Chapter 1; and in their concluding section they refer to the (neglected) issue of ownership and control (see the 'democracy' perspective in Chapter 1). If the regenerative power of culture is to be fully realised, then these issues of ownership and control must be addressed.

In Chapter 3, *Corporate Governance and Ethics*, Philip Stiles does address this issue from the angle of corporate governance. This is less a question of pure ownership, and more one of control and accountability. Stiles examines two key areas: the relationship between the board and the shareholders, and the relationship of the board with the shareholders to society as a whole. If the board should set the ethical framework within which the company operates, then how is this significant role to be achieved? With unitary boards (the German system of two-tier boards seems a non-starter), non-executive directors are always caught in the paradox of having to be involved enough in the company to ask searching questions, but also to maintain adequate distance and independence. This has led to calls for greater shareholder involvement in running the company, but such interventions are often only at the extremes, and too little too late. In terms of the relationship with society, the stakeholder model is taken as given, and critically examined. This requires greater disclosure of information and representation (the ownership question again) if it is to work – something fiercely resisted by companies. This all leads to the question: *self-regulation, or legislation?* It seems the former will prevail if companies are seen politically to act legitimately in the public's eyes. In the final analysis, Stiles suggests the effectiveness of corporate governance still rests on the integrity of the people involved – a virtue ethics approach (see Chapter 1).

In Chapter 4, *Business and its Social Responsibility*, Andrew Wilson takes the notion of a company's 'licence to operate' as a way of investigating the role and legitimacy of business activity. Discerning customers, jobseekers, investors and employees are all creating a changed external environment which companies ignore at their peril. The argument that the growing number of 'ethical consumers' and 'ethical investors' continues to put pressure on companies to behave more responsibly seems sound enough. The argument that 'discerning jobseekers' who are concerned to work only for companies with a good ethical reputation seems initially less persuasive in a time of high unemployment, but inexorable demographic changes, coupled with the cost to companies of not recruiting the right people of high calibre who stay for a reasonable length of time, suggest that this will be an increasingly important factor in the future. Changing employee expectations also mean that companies are going to have to 'walk the talk' about people being their greatest asset, and develop organisational cultures that engender fairness and respect if they are to get any company loyalty in return. All this, Andrew Wilson suggests, lends support to the argument that (in the long term) good ethics is good business; without it, companies will lose their licence to operate.

If there is any validity in the democratic process, then the public's assessment of the role and legitimacy of business will, sooner or later, be reflected in changes in the law, and changes in the values and attitudes of business people. The discussion in Part I is essentially grappling with the implications of the stakeholder model of business. How accountable is a manager to the various stakeholders? How can that accountability be practically realised? What power should the various stakeholders have in relation to the activities of businesses? These questions are all being asked in a climate of changing expectations for greater transparency and clearer accountability. No doubt the debate will rage on, but it is difficult to see how far such issues can be resolved without opening up the question of ownership (financial, as well as conceptual). Indeed, the ownership question is closely related to motivation and therefore underlies many of the chapters in Part II.

1

BUSINESS PHILOSOPHY
Searching for an authentic role
Peter W. F. Davies

INTRODUCTION

Much of the debate about the various issues in business ethics is fuelled by implicit and differing philosophies of business. Clearly, if you believe that the basic role of business is 'to maximise profit', then your analysis of business ethics issues will differ considerably from that of those who assume that the basic role of business is 'to provide meaningful employment'. Not only do such hidden assumptions undermine the value of the business ethics debate, but the danger of such generally teleological approaches is that they may focus too much on *ends*, with the *means* getting less-than-adequate emphasis. Philosophy equally addresses *both*, by asking two fundamental questions of any phenomenon which is the subject of its investigation; its *meaning*, and its *purpose*. Put into the context of business activity these roughly translate into:

1 What is the meaning of business (activity)?
2 What purpose is in it (if any)?

This chapter looks at the second question first, via an examination of five differing ethical perspectives of modern-day business, and then attempts to draw out both the meaning of business in relation to each perspective, and also the implications for business ethics theory from each of the differing views. My own bias is a belief that the historical context is very important; what has gone before in large measure shapes our current understanding in the world of ideas, as well as shaping the physical world. For business, this influence of the past cannot be fully understood without due appreciation of developments in technology.[1]

15

A WESTERN CHRISTIAN THEOLOGICAL PERSPECTIVE

In the West we have been deeply affected by Christianity in our understanding of all areas of life, including business. The starting point for a Christian understanding of business as a cultural activity would normally be Niebuhr's classic on Christian social ethics, *Christ and Culture*.[2] Niebuhr's five archetypal answers each lead to differing understandings of the meaning and purpose of business, so I will focus here on aspects widely accepted in the Christian tradition. God, it is believed, has a purpose for every individual's life, which includes the cultural collective contexts of those lives, such as business activity. Recently however, Christianity has been severely blamed by environmentalists for business's exploitative attitudes towards nature (the ecology) which (it is claimed) the Christian religion has sanctioned.[3] This has been due to Christianity's emphasis on human beings as the pinnacle of creation, and on the afterlife, and these two are held responsible for desacralising and debasing the value of nature in the here and now, hence sanctioning business short-termism. Such an accusation, though, is based on a narrow interpretation of Genesis 1:28 ('And God said unto them . . . have dominion over . . . '[4]). Perhaps also, historically, the Protestant Work Ethic at its worst *could* be said to have sanctioned *any* work (however dangerous and demeaning) as of value in God's eyes, as well as ignoring the pollution of the Industrial Revolution. In more recent years the Church has countered this with its green credentials,[5] focusing on God's mandate for man *to sustainably develop the earth's potential* (' . . . to dress it and keep it . . . ' and ' . . . to work it and take care of it . . . '[6]). Due reference is also made to good treatment of animals, just relations, and the golden rule. The implication of all this is that (some negative experiences notwithstanding) business is still a key, God-ordained activity, a calling of high esteem, and should be seen in terms of being a *vocation*.

A second important aspect concerns the implications of the Fall. Although business should not be seen as a necessary evil, the ground *was* cursed (Genesis 3:17–19), and from that point on economic activity (mainly agriculture) was to become a never-ending harsh grind, instead of a joyous creative activity. The point here is that economy is fundamentally about *work*, not *money* (even though money is the usual language of discussion – witness the fact that unemployment seems no longer to be given much prominence as a key issue). This suggests that a shift in emphasis is needed in assess-

16

ing the value of a business in terms of *work provided*, rather than by some abstract financial measure.

A third lesson is that humans are *made in the image of God*. There is an inherent dignity in every human being that must be respected. Businesses should therefore avoid dangerous, debilitating and alienating work, *not* because it might be bad for business, but because humans are made in God's image; it is an end in itself, rather than a means to an end. Such a view is of course part of Kant's thinking, as well as being reflected in the Universal Declaration of Human Rights.

The above three points suggest a different understanding of business's meaning and purpose. Here the debate seems to surround Colossians 1:19–20 – 'reconciling all things'.[7] This points towards the importance of *justice* in work relations within and between business organisations, and the fact that the whole of business activity, from design, to manufacture, to distribution of goods (and services), should reflect the theme of reconciliation.[8]

The emphasis of this section has been to counterbalance the more usual *individualist* interpretations of Christianity (i.e. you can work in an armaments factory with a clear conscience, as long as you are a clean-living, honest, productive worker), and to emphasise the broader and longer-term structural theological understanding which informs the 'true' purpose of business activity – a means of reconciliation, just (re)distribution, and providing dignified work. From this theological perspective, business (as God's work) should be viewed much more as a *vocation* and ranked seriously as a *profession* of very high standing; if this were so, then perhaps better behaviour would be expected, and delivered. It is against such criteria that the ethics of any business should be assessed.

AN (INDUSTRIAL) DEMOCRACY PERSPECTIVE

It seems to be generally agreed that democracy is *a good thing*; and since the collapse of communism (the better system has prevailed, good has triumphed over the *Evil Empire*,[9] etc.), it is now assumed that capitalism is also *a good thing*. It is essential for democracy, and vice versa. But with communism apparently out of the way, attention has shifted to scrutinise capitalism and democracy more critically. For example, it is now more openly noted (also fuelled by the debate about the extent of Britain's involvement in the EC) that capitalism, and its handmaiden *the market system*, can vary considerably between countries, witness the difference between Japan, Germany, Sweden and the UK.[10] These different countries highlight also the variations of democracy at work *in industry*, as well as in national politics. The 'democracy' issue appears to be debated on two (inter-linked) fronts. First, that without increased industrial democracy there is a broader threat to the survival of democracy at the national level[11] (e.g. unregulated multinational companies (MNCs) are the new, up and coming 'nation-states'[12]), and second, that more democracy is required within business organisations both for ends (e.g. greater employee motivation), and as a good thing *per se*.[13] Differing levels of acceptance of these two issues also affect presuppositions about the role of business, and what are considered to be ethical issues in business.

To understand the arguments about industrial democracy it helps to look briefly at how companies (business organisations) have developed in terms of the law. In the period between the fifteenth and seventeenth centuries, work was based around the guilds, which had the responsibility to oversee issues such as quality and fair dealing. In the seventeenth and eighteenth centuries, the guilds collapsed, and incorporation as a 'chartered company' was enabled by an Act of Parliament. This allowed certain monopolistic powers (against the abuse of which Adam Smith argued), but 'incorporation' was nevertheless encouraged on the understanding that it *should serve a public purpose*; it was for public profit, not private gain.[14] The earliest companies were family owned and run, and were small in scale not just due to distribution logistics, but because there was *un*limited liability. A bankruptcy could throw into poverty an entire family, and hence not surprisingly was a severe disincentive to entrepreneurial activity. With the advent of *limited* liability in the mid-nineteenth century,[15] companies could grow in size without limit, and the second half of the Industrial Revolution saw massive expansion as a result. At first, when families took advantage of limited liability, nothing much changed, since they continued to own and run the companies. But when a company grew into a joint-stock company, with shares being bought and sold on the London Stock Exchange, ownership was separated from responsibility. Shareholders, bearing no relation to each other (except in their desire for profit), had no sense of responsibility for the firm's employees, nor for the local community within which the firm operated. This divorce of ownership from responsibility has become maximised in the multinational company, and is reflected in the differing rewards between those who contribute the capital and those who 'merely' contribute their work.[16]

It is argued that the outcome of all this is: alienated, demotivated employees who have no positive reason to be loyal to the company; short-termism, particularly in the case of shareholders and city investors; and a managerial elite which acts as if it owns the company and which wields massive, unchecked powers. Company law, designed for the previous century, has remained essentially unchanged despite the Companies Act of 1980 and the subsequent consolidating Act of 1985. There is no commonality of purpose for those involved in the enterprise, and this (it is argued) is dangerous for democracy.

The implication of this for business ethics is that ethics should be reflected in changing company law, both for the internal control and accountability of businesses, as well as their global regulation. The first point is addressed under the heading of *Corporate Governance*, with, for example, the notion of directors as trustees being reintroduced, and the Cadbury report goes some way in this respect.[17] From a 'democracy' point of view, the global regulation of MNCs is important, because democracy depends for its survival on a number of *intermediate* institutions (e.g. the judiciary), and no single one of them must be allowed to become too powerful; MNCs have become 'unnatural' for a democratic society. From this perspective the purpose of business organisations is (in their provision of goods and services) to support democracy by letting the people have power in their internal affairs, by encouraging them to be involved in 'citizenship' duties, and in their overall regulation. By criteria such as these they should therefore be ethically evaluated.

AN (ECO)SYSTEMS PERSPECTIVE

The environmental movement was essentially founded in 1962 with the publication of Rachel Carson's *Silent Spring*.[18] Since then, business has fought tooth and nail virtually every new piece of legislation concerning the reduction and control of industrial pollution. But what has become clearer in the last thirty-plus years is that, through the power of technology (which is organised by business), humans have become a major planetary force.[19] Whether we like it or not, we are being forced to be stewards of the whole of creation, not just of all human, animal and vegetable life, but also of the biosphere and of planetary survival. From the Goddess Gaia and the Butterfly Effect, to research into weather prediction and endangered species, it is gradually being accepted that the world is one fragile, interactive and interdependent system in which the activities of business organisations can be seen to be severely dysfunctional and even threatening to the survival of the human race. The industrial system (in its present form) has come hard up against the ecological system, and both cannot win.

In recent years, organisation theorists have examined organisations as machines, as political systems, as cultures, as brains (the learning organisation), as psychic prisons, and as organisms.[20] The last of these, as organisms adapting to a hostile environment, has most relevance here. It raises an issue deeply rooted in the human psyche, that of reducing the uncertainties of living with the unpredictable vagaries of nature. The answer is seen in technology, as the means to gain control over nature (as well as usefully freeing us from sweated labour to provide the basic necessities of life). But technology is a little-understood beast which, even when used for good ends, appears to have an ambivalent nature with negative side-effects which often are only discovered years, or decades, later. So it appears that we have replaced the uncertainties of nature with the uncertainties of technology. If it takes several years to find out that something as simple as a chlorofluorocarbon (CFC) can punch holes in the ozone layer, what hope have we with genetic engineering and nano-technology?

Whether you believe we need *more* technology to solve our problems (the technology fix), or *less* (alternative technology), both camps agree that powerful businesses and their technologies are a detrimental organism in the overall ecosystem, and more of a cancer than a parasite. One suggestion is to increase the biodiversity of business organisations by decreasing their size.[21] The call comes not just from ecologists, but also from writers on strategy who see large organisations as potential dinosaurs.[22] In other words, *there appear to be natural laws for the long-term survival both of businesses and of the planet, and they are complementary.* The implications of chaos theory, and the continual flux and transformation that underlie what were perceived to be constant phenomena, suggest that (after 200 years of 'normal' science) we may be entering a period of 'revolutionary' science[23] in which there is a major paradigm shift in the basic framework of how we understand the world, and hence what is real, and consequently how we determine our priorities.

The implication of all this is that business's overriding and primary ethical task is both to avoid any further damage to the ecosystem, and to start repairs, and against these criteria business should be judged.[24] But even the most cursory glance at business history will reveal that business generally has a short-term view, and hence is unlikely to do much of what, as suggested here, is required until forced to do so by law. However, the ecosystem view requires a *global* perspective, but the difficulties in getting any *international* agreement on such laws, let alone enforcing them, is well known, and raises one of the most difficult questions facing business ethics today: by what authority *can*, as well as should, global business activity be regulated? The ecosystems perspective *demands* that this question be tackled as a matter of global urgency, since, even if the 'dinosaur' theorists are right, it may be too late by the time business organisation organisms attain the required level of self-realisation to repair the impact of their activities.

A FRIEDMANITE, 'THE BUSINESS OF BUSINESS IS BUSINESS', PERSPECTIVE

In the twenty-five-plus years since Milton Friedman published his seminal 1970 article *The Social Responsibility of Business is to Increase its Profits,*[25] he has had his followers in method, as well as in content. The basic method is to define very tightly what is legitimately the territory and role of business (as opposed to that of government, charities, trade associations, etc.), and then to go on to 'solve' business ethics problems using the tight definition. Using this approach, one can therefore dismiss a number of business ethics problems simply by saying they are the responsibility of government (or whoever) and not of business. A particularly well-argued example of this genre is Elaine Sternberg's *Just Business.*[26] She defines the purpose of business as being *to maximise owner value over the long term by selling goods or services* subject to the process of doing business being within the two ethical norms of *distributive justice and common decency.*[27] The mechanism of a tight definition then leads to a four-step ethical decision model which, she claims, 'can resolve business ethics problems in all their current variety, and as they arise in new and unanticipated forms'.[28]

There are several problems with such an approach. First, of course, is whether you accept the definitions in the first place. Often this has to do with how broad an approach to stakeholder theory is taken. The traditional approach of shareholders as owners getting their due has long been questioned, but still holds sway. Second, the define-tightly-then-logically-apply method can be a useful tool in philosophical logic, helping to keep arguments generally sound, but tends to close down options, whereas the nature of ethics is to explore right and wrong, good and bad, in a changing world, and hence to open things up. Third, this approach also invites the problematic of viewing business as a separate 'game' with its own rules, etc. The danger of this in business ethics is that business in particular is a very pervasive and powerful activity in the lives of most individuals in society, and therefore cannot be divorced from its impact on (innocent) bystanders; a more integrative approach makes better sense in this context.[29] Fourth, leaving remedial medicine to the actions of individuals, pressure groups and government does not adequately take into account the asymmetrical power relations between business and these other groupings (especially in an imperfect market system), nor does it deal adequately with the time lag in getting regulation in place, an issue increasingly crucial in an ever faster-changing world.

The implications of this perspective for business ethics is that it usefully highlights the danger of loose talk in business ethics. Any definition immediately provides both new insights into this emerging field, and also closes out other ways of seeing things. Business ethics from this perspective should be assessed by such criteria as the persuasiveness of the definitions, and the logic with which they are applied.

A VIRTUES PERSPECTIVE

Much of the business ethics literature is written from the standpoint of 'doing' rather than that of 'being', and this leads to an approach based on applying ethical theories to business situations, often with lots of case studies and an ethical algorithm to help managers resolve the myriad of tortuous ethical dilemmas of which they have newly become aware.[30] The emphasis on practicality is to be expected (and to some extent applauded) when academic philosophers are attempting to convey the relevance of their subject to a wide audience of action-oriented managers, suspicious of both academics and ethics.

But, according to the virtues approach, these attempts are fundamentally flawed because essentially you can go no further than merely expose centuries-old debates between differing philosophical schools, (e.g. if you are a Kantian you should do this; if you are an Act Utilitarian you should do that). Virtue business ethics is both a very new, and an important, addition to business ethics theory; and a pioneering text here is Robert Solomon's *Ethics and Excellence*.[31] It draws on the Aristotelian notion of 'virtue', and thereby focuses on the *character* of people in business organisations. The assumption is that, by definition, business is not a legalistic fiction, but a holistic practice, a social activity whose purpose is 'to provide essential and desirable goods – to make life easier',[32] and that the business organisation itself is 'a community (within larger communities) and . . . a culture with shared values and larger concerns'.[33] Business ethics is, therefore, 'not the superimposition of foreign values in business but the understanding of the foundations of business itself'.[34] The notion of sacrificing profits for social responsibility, therefore, is a misnomer, because '[s]ocial responsibility only means that the purpose of business is to do what business has always been meant to do, enrich society as well as the pockets of those who are responsible for the enriching'.[35] Likewise, money spent on being a caring organisation is not, as Milton Friedman might suggest, 'theft' from the shareholders; rather, 'the ultimate aim of the Aristotelian approach to business is to cultivate whole human beings, not jungle fighters, efficiency automatons, or "good soldiers"'.[36]

The outcome of all this is that business is fundamentally about *relationships*, and how we relate to each other depends on the virtuous nature of our characters. Without honesty, fairness and trust, business transactions would just never take place; without friendliness, honour and loyalty, business organisations themselves would fall apart. Without justice, the legitimacy and effectiveness of business collapses.[37] For Solomon, keeping the big picture in mind, and avoiding moral myopia, is essential for good business practice and decision-making. This requires moral courage, both to see and to do the right thing (to maintain integrity) in face of the acute 'moral mazes' of life, perhaps felt especially strongly in most business organisations.[38] Business ethics, therefore, should move away from techniques for applying ethical theory via an ethical algorithm, since such techniques are misplaced and reveal a misunderstanding of the essential nature of business. The focus on ethics and excellence, on character and virtues, on community, is not a means to the end of efficiency and effectiveness, but constitutes the very heart and soul of business activity. But, as Solomon admits, 'character' is set in the early days of youth, and no business ethics module taken later on in higher education is likely to change it. The purpose of business ethics, then, becomes a focus on how business can reinvent itself in the light of personal character development. The key question is: will it make better men and women? In the forty years of organisational impact on our 'working' lives, what kind of women and men do we want to become? The virtues perspective suggests, then, that it is in the light of such questions that business activity should be ethically evaluated.

CONCLUSIONS

The five preceding perspectives have, in turn, pointed towards the meaning and purpose of business as essentially being a God-ordained vocation, a crucial element in democracy, a key element in the planetary ecosystem, a financial wealth creator, and a forum to develop people. Are these perspectives mutually exclusive? I think not; one can see elements of all of them in most businesses, but at various times in history, and in various geo-political contexts, one perspective may become over-emphasised and hence other perspectives have to be championed in order for them to be put on the agenda at all.

The Friedmanite worldview of business and society has had a long innings at the top, but as an entrenched paradigm its validity is increasingly being questioned. That is not to say it is about to be toppled by other perspectives, but the other four all point towards a broadening out (a stakeholder model) of both the values that drive business, and the legal and organisational frameworks in which they operate. If there are any natural laws in the Universe, then it seems reasonable to expect that over the *next* twenty-five years or so, the Friedmanite followers will have at the very least to 'walk the talk' of other views, whether it be in the language of vocation, ecology, democracy, virtues, or some new language yet to re-emerge from the deep historical (and oft forgotten) legacy of philosophical discourse.

NOTES

1 Staudenmaier, John M., SJ (1985) *Technology's Storytellers: Reweaving the Human Fabric*, Cambridge, Mass: MIT Press and The Society for the History of Technology.

2 Niebuhr, H. Richard (1951) *Christ and Culture*, New York: Harper and Row. Niebuhr distinguishes five typical understandings in which the Christian can relate to cultural activities: Christ against Culture, The Christ of Culture, Christ above Culture, Christ and Culture in Paradox, and Christ the Transformer of Culture.

3 A seminal article in this respect was: *White, Lynn, Jr* (1967) 'The Historical Roots of our Ecological Crisis', *Science*, 155 (10 March), pp. 1203–7. Also published in the same year as 'St Francis and the Ecologic Backlash', in *Horizon*, 9(3), pp. 42–7.

4 This translation is from the Authorised Version of the Bible.

5 Bradley, Ian (1990) *God is Green*, London: Darton, Longman & Todd.

6 Genesis 2:15; quoting from the Authorised Version and the New International Version respectively.

7 The full text in the New International Version reads:

For God was pleased to have all his fullness dwell in him [Christ], and through him to reconcile all things, whether things on earth or things in heaven, by making peace through his blood, shed on the cross.

8 These ideas also stem from workshops I was involved in during the mid-1980s under the auspices of Christian Industrial Enterprises Ltd.

9 The phrase *The Evil Empire* was used by US President Ronald Reagan as a description of the communist Soviet bloc, headed by Russia.

10 Hampden-Turner, Charles, and Trompenaars, Fons (1994) *The Seven Cultures of Capitalism: (Value-Systems for Creating Wealth in the United States, Britain, Japan, Germany, France, Sweden and the Netherlands)*, London: Piatkus.

11 Goyder, George (1993) *The Just Enterprise: A Blueprint for the Responsible Company*, London: Adamantine Press.

12 Naisbitt, John (1995) *Global Paradox: The bigger the world economy, the more powerful its smallest players*, Brealey Publishing.

13 Parkyn, Brian (1979) *Democracy, Accountability and Participation in Industry*, Bradford: MCB Publications.

14 Goyder, *The Just Enterprise*, p. 17.

15 Limited Liability was first enacted in 1855, and consolidated in the Companies Act of 1862; see Goyder, *The Just Enterprise*.

16 Goyder, *The Just Enterprise*, pp. 18–19.

17 For a brief summary of the Cadbury Report see Cannon, Tom (1994) *Corporate Responsibility: A Textbook on Business Ethics, Governance, Environment: Roles and Responsibilities*, London: Pitman.

18 Carson, Rachel (1962) *Silent Spring*, Harmondsworth: Penguin.

19 Davies, Peter W. F. (1995) 'Managing Technology: Some Ethical Preliminaries', *Business Ethics: A European Review*, 4(3), pp. 130–8.

20 Morgan, Gareth (1986) *Images of Organization*, New York: Sage.

21 Hawken, Paul (1993) *The Ecology of Commerce: (How business can save the planet)*, London: Weidenfeld & Nicolson.

22 For example, see Stacey, Ralph D. (1993) *Strategic Management and Organisational Dynamics*, London: Pitman.

23 Kuhn, Thomas S. (1970) *The Structure of Scientific Revolutions*, Chicago: University of Chicago Press (1st edn, 1962). See also Sheldrake, Rupert (1994) *Seven Experiments that Could Change the World: (A do-it-yourself guide to revolutionary science)*, London: Fourth Estate.

24 Hawken, *The Ecology of Commerce*.

25 Friedman, Milton (1970) 'The Social Responsibility of Business is to Increase its Profits', *New York Sunday Times Magazine*, 13 September, pp. 32 *et seq.*; widely reprinted since.

26 Sternberg, Elaine (1994) *Just Business: Business Ethics in Action*. London: Little Brown & Co.

27 Sternberg, *Just Business*, p. 32, pp. 79–87.

28 Ibid., p. 5.

29 Jeurissen, R. (1995) *Business in Response to the Morally Concerned Public*, in Van Luijk, H. and Ulrich, P. (eds), *Facing Public Interest: Ethical Challenge to Business Policy and Corporate Communications*, Dordrecht: Kluwer Academic Publishers.

30 For example, see Clutterbuck, David, *et al.* (1992) *Actions Speak Louder: A Management Guide to Corporate Social Responsibility*, London: Kogan Page (and Kingfisher); Green, Ronald M. (1993) *The Ethical Manager: A New Method for Business Ethics*, New York: Macmillan; Hall, William D. (1993) *Making the Right Decision: Ethics for Managers*, New York: Wiley; Snell, Robin (1993) *Developing Skills for Ethical Management*, London: Chapman & Hall.

31 Solomon, Robert C. (1993) *Ethics and Excellence: Co-operation and Integrity in Business* (The Ruffin Series in Business Ethics), New York: Oxford University Press.

32 Solomon, *Ethics and Excellence*, p. 118.

33 Ibid., p. 133.

34 Ibid., p. 6.

35 Ibid., pp. 180–1.

36 Ibid., p. 180.

37 Ibid., see chapters 20, 21 and 22.

38 See Jackall, Robert (1988) *Moral Mazes: The World of Corporate Managers*, New York: Oxford University Press.

2

WHOSE BUSINESS IS IT ANYWAY?

The question of sustainability

Raff Carmen and Marek Lubelski

INTRODUCTION

The international project of development, proclaimed at the inaugural address of US President Truman in 1949 as 'a bold new program for making the benefits of our scientific advances and industrial progress available for the improvement and growth of the underdeveloped areas'[1] has increasingly been exposed as the reality of global *maldevelopment*. By way of describing its ethical basis and cultural effects, it has been branded 'the new colonialism' and 'the project of Western patriarchy'.[2] At the same time, among the industrialised countries, the recognition of a looming environmental crisis in particular has impressed upon public consciousness the hitherto unthinkable – namely, that the North, too, must develop itself.[3] The discussion that follows aims to show that questions of *business's future sustainability* are askable only in the context of this debate over the ethics and consequence of what is generally called 'development'. Sachs,[4] among others, points to the 'amoeba'-like quality of the word, in the sense that it has no fixed boundary and is subject to radically differing interpretations, at the same time as emphasising its indispensability. Given that we cannot but progress and change in both North and South, the key questions remain as to what the nature of that change ought to be, what kind of development should we choose, and what are our reasons for making that choice. Whatever the choices, though, business organisations, due to their power as shapers and agents of social change, need to be called to account and evaluated according to these macro-ethical considerations.

GENUINE SUSTAINABLILITY V. COMPETITIVE, 'BUSINESS IS BUSINESS', SURVIVAL

Within both governmental and non-governmental organisations, the idea of 'sustainable' development has appeared of late as a lodestar for orienting policy and strategy alike. Whether North or South, the environmental and social consequences of our actions are coming to light – demographic explosions combined with increasing global and social inequality and conflict, exacerbated by massive natural resource depletion and compounded by the effects of industrial waste and pollution. This adds up to a highly unstable equation on a comparatively short timescale, one where the future of our entire human culture is measured against the ecological and social systems on which it depends.[5] Military economics and the unabated trade in the hardware of destruction remain the ultimate comment on the multi-faceted paradox of maldevelopment. Some degree of recognition of the unsustainable nature of 'our common future' is becoming apparent across the widest spectrum of perspectives – from Nepalese hill farmers to the chief executives of major petrochemical corporations.

The quest for genuine and holistic responses to our predicament, which previously had been more characteristic of citizens' associations networks and local pressure groups, has now been projected on to the global political scene with the 1992 Rio Earth Summit and the United Nations Conference on Environment and Development process (UNCED). This has committed the leaders of more than 170 nations to producing and enacting a global agenda for the twenty-first century (Agenda 21) which aims to ensure environmental and social sustainability. In essence, this means that the idea of 'sustainability' is no longer solely an element of the discourse of social change and reform, but a language that appears to be common to both government and citizen, powerful and dispossessed, North and South. This apparent commonality, however, masks ethical and intellectual differences of the most basic nature which are critically important in any evaluation of the ethics of business enterprise.

As a result of, and linked to, the political developments outlined above, the business sector, although traditionally the last to respond to issues of this nature (due most probably to its being the first to be implicated in their causes), has begun to register a certain willingness to come to grips with the personal and professional implica-

28

tions of those developments in the destruction of the social and nat-ural environment. International initiatives, such as the International Chamber of Commerce (ICC)'s Commission on the Environment 'Business Approach to Sustainable Development',[6] and the Business Council for Sustainable Development (BCSD)'s 'Changing Course',[7] have indicated an attempt to show that economic develop-ment and environmental sustainability can be integrated to ensure 'quality of life' through a voluntary approach to corporate good practice. More recently, in an obvious sequel to the Club of Rome's 'Limits to Growth',[8] eighteen intellectuals and researchers from Europe, North America and Japan, known as 'the group of Lisbon', under the direction of Riccardo Petrella, warn against the globalisa-tion ('triadisation', i.e. North America, Europe and Japan) of busi-ness and trade,[9] putting into question the 'gospel of Competition'.[10] This dogma of competition, having pervaded all spheres of life and not just the world of business alone, makes no economic, ecological, social nor, ultimately, ethical 'sense', and is ill-equipped to act as a universal principle to rule the planet.

Such perspectives on business and development have emerged as a growing, though diverse, ethical critique of what has come to be known as the dominant 'business-of-business-is-business' paradigm. At one level, this critique focuses on damage limitation. A case in point is the revealing subtitle of one of the Institute of Business Ethics (IBE)'s more recent publications: 'Case studies of Cost Savings and New Opportunities from Environmental Initiatives'.[11] Sustainablity is presented here almost entirely as a function of main-stream corporate practice's relentless progress through a market economy. Sound environmental management, while offering some welcome first tentative steps for organisations beginning to analyse and reduce their environmental impact or 'footprint', is nevertheless primarily rooted in a model of business management which is cul-turally and historically specific, where 'eco-efficiency' relates first and foremost to a *company's*, rather than the general public's, need for survival. The limitations of such approaches, and the shallow-ness of the moral principle invoked, are highlighted by Paul Hawken, when he points out that 'even if every company on the planet were to adopt the best environmental practices of the leading companies – say the Body Shop, Patagonia, or 3M – the world would still be moving towards sure degradation and collapse'.[12]

As Lao Tsu suggested, several hundred years BC in China, ethics only appears on the scene when something has gone wrong at a deeper level.[13] Progressive tendencies within business ethics remain predicated on a worldview that arose from and fed on a history of massive human and natural exploitation[14] and which now offers a hopeless exclusion to the vast majority of the planet's population, while continuing to sell a fantasy of endless consumable wants (desires) made from allegedly inexhaustible resources. From this perspective, it is understandable why indigenous peoples represented at the Rio Summit observed that the whole process 'seemed to function like a commercial market-place . . . poor countries of the South selling their natural resources, including human beings, to the highest bidder'.[15] Middleton *et al.* concur that the real agenda of Rio, like the tears of a crocodile, had less to do with genuine concern for the environment than with preserving the interests of the North at the expense not only of the natural world and its resources but also of the peoples of the so-called developing world.[16] The question of sustainability, in the light of these considerations, becomes a question of the ownership of the nature, purpose and direction of development. The predecessors and progenitors of ethical systems – the wisdom-based knowledge systems of the East as well as those of indigenous cultures the world over – were organised around principles of human need; 'What would happen' asks Eduardo Galeano, 'if the whole population of the South devoured the world just as unpunished as the North and with the same voracity?'[17] If business ethics as a field of knowledge and guiding principle for reformative action is to contribute to the resolution of such problems of the concentration of ownership and control, it will have to go beyond the closed-circuit of 'business-is-business' logic and start to look for and evaluate *genuine* alternatives.

FROM 'HOW TO HAVE MORE' TO 'HOW MUCH IS ENOUGH?'

Cultural determinism is so powerful that it is very difficult politically to admit that economic growth (with all its connotations of ultimate goodness – the modern substitute for the Ancients' '*summum bonum*'), must be limited. Universal wisdom holds that less growth (and hence less consumption) will seriously undermine the economic system; and yet it is imperative that the basic assumptions underlying industrial society change both fundamentally, and now (preferably, starting with the North). The problem facing the future world is not how to encourage more competition and growth, but how to stop the spiral of universal maldevelopment in both North and South. The key question which increasingly will have to be asked and answered in the future by rich and poor countries alike is: 'How much is enough?'[18] In recent years, CEPAUR (the Centre for Urban and Rural Development in Chile) has done pioneering work on the verification of a 'threshold' hypothesis. This holds that, in any society, there is a period of time in which an increase in GNP (Gross National Product – economic growth, conventionally measured) will bring about a positive and measurable increase in the quality of life of people, hence the 'Quality of Life Index' (QLI).[19] The 'threshold' is the point beyond which any further growth will result in a deterioration of people's quality of life. The relevance and accuracy of this hypothesis, even in purely economic terms, has been confirmed in the meantime by the independent work of Daly and Cobb.[20] Their 'Index of Sustainable Economic Welfare' (ISEW) confirms that, in the case of the US for example, the growth of GNP ran parallel with a growth in quality of life. But, starting from 1974–75, with growth still continuing, the ISEW started to decline. The question is crucial because, when things start taking a turn for the worse, they cannot possibly be improved with politicians' current cure-all palliative of yet more economic growth and a competitive free-for-all.

Current business thinking, idioms and training modules, embedded as they are in a vision of development wedded to 'the expansion of the flow of consumption', are ill-suited to the challenges posed by sustainability and the ethical and practical demands of changing from a consumerist to a creativist culture. The satisfaction of human need is not primary, nor is achievement of ecological balance paramount.[21] This is clear from an examination of management buzzwords currently in vogue: 're-engineering' does not address the problematic of superfluous and inappropriate production, nor that of the exploitative nature of disproportionate extraction from Third World countries. 'Downsizing' does not include, as it should, a genuine commitment to smaller, more regionally-based human-scale enterprises geared to local regeneration. 'The learning organisation' *ought* to indicate corporations which, having drawn lessons from past environmental malpractice and recognising the crisis of sustainability, have now the courage to make radical social change an integral part of their mission statements and corporate practice. What is clearly crucial in realising business's role in the process of development is the semiology of the language used, and the ethics and perceptions that are deployed at the initial moment of defining that process. Returning for a moment to the Ancients, Aristotle drew the famous distinction between *chrematistics* and *oikonomia*, where the former involves the manipulation of the household to increase wealth for short-term profit, while the latter refers to the sound management of the household to increase its benefit in the future. As Daly and Cobb point out, the 'household' really describes 'the larger community of the land, of shared values, resources, biomass, institutions, language and history'.[22] This is where economics and ecology literally meet and share a common home in the root 'oikos', and where the distinction between truly sustainable and ultimately unsustainable perspectives becomes clear. Sustainability of economics and of the ecology meet when people join to 'humanise the landscape'.[23]

THE CULTURE OF POWER AND THE POWER OF CULTURE: THE GLOBAL CIVIC SOCIETY AND SUSTAINABLE DEVELOPMENT

Present global maldevelopment, then, has largely come about as a result of the untrammelled concentration of wealth and power in the hands of those who direct it – 'First' and 'Third' Worlds are not geographical, but political, concepts – and the victims of this depletion of resources are the previously self-sustaining local systems. This typically involves extraction of their mineral wealth, reduction of their biomass (biodiversity) and obliteration of their local knowledge systems (cultural diversity). Further to this extractive and exploitative relationship, dominant development processes have promoted the commoditisation and commercialisation of the physical landscape, which still leaves people in predominantly agricultural economies increasingly deprived of their access to nature and, therefore, increasingly dependent on the economic system brought about by those processes. As noted above, the crisis of sustainability has given rise to what the Lisbon Group calls 'the new enlightened elites', those at the cutting edge of the 'new global civic society' who are working to articulate critiques of and alternatives to maldevelopment and business's part in it. But this global civic society also has its counterparts at the grassroots. There are, at the present moment, 'approximately 450,000 interest groups and non-government organisations throughout the world. A very large proportion have a "globalist", planetary and international outlook. They represent between 600 and 800 million members and supporters with approximately 5 to 6 million leaders.'[24] The Third World Network, the International Foundation for Development Alternatives (IFDA, Nyon, Switzerland), the Cultures Network (Brussels), and the African Network of Indigenous Environment and Development, are just a few examples of a world-encompassing network of organisations researching and rooted in such local initiatives and people-centred activism for sustainability.

Their contribution to this debate is marked by their overriding concern for social equity, justice and cultural autonomy, elements which are all too easily overlooked by ethical perspectives that emphasise economic and ethnocentric concerns.[25] However much the economic scene may be dominated by the culture of competition and the culture of power, it is the power of culture, as embodied in the goals and methods of such organisations, whether traditional or newly-formed, which will continue to be the wellspring of human-scale economics and development. The microdynamics of the *popular economy* – because that is what, positively speaking, the economist's 'Informal sector' really is – operate and proliferate with little reference (and often in contradiction) to the imperatives of the formal, *organised* economy. It is characterised by a mixture (*métissage*)[26] of local cultures and technologies with a certain amount of outside imports which, after assimilation, take on an entirely localised character within a human scale. This renders them virtually immune to the economics of competition and universalist development.

What we are emphasising here is the co-existence of two entirely different economic practices which stem from disparate cultural understandings of economics and, by implication, of society and development itself. As the unitary 'New World Order' of competitive enterprise is being imposed with increasing vigour, and as this world is more and more converging towards the bland point zero of a uniform 'global village', it will increasingly, and quite naturally in cultural terms, be resisted: a resistance and a rebellion – sometimes identified negatively as 'cultural lag' by anthropologists – which owes nothing to economic rationality or logic, but which has everything to do with cultural identity, autonomous reflection and human agency. Popular resistance and popular ingenuity have been a constant obstacle to the march of modernity, which makes its inroads largely on the back, and at the expense, of self-sufficient cultures. But this resistance also continues because no impositions can ever prevent economic and social life from continuing to (re)invent itself. The essence of development does indeed not reside in the satisfaction of a proliferation of needs. The essence of development is not provision, but *creation*. And creation – 'the art of making something out of nothing' – lies at the heart of the meaning of culture.

Interventionist development, on the other hand, is mediated by what could be described as development 'packages', prepared in the forwarding ('developed') countries for transfer to or promotion and sale in the 'developing' world. With the loss of access to and control over support systems, formerly held in common, and with the depletion of biological, cultural and other forms of diversity, as well as the loss of local knowledges, comes the breakdown of the family as the focus of social reproduction. Collapse of the environment and collapse of community upon itself go hand in hand: one will not long outlast the other. It is interesting to note how the pattern of maldevelopment outlined here has already been enacted in the histories of 'developed' cultures' relationships to themselves. Development practice that fails to recognise such cultural groundings will inevitably wreak havoc on its 'target' populations. Similarly, Western-style management and enterprise training modules, targeted matter-of-factly at developing country audiences, are symptomatic of a general climate of spoon-fed dependence on alien societal and instructional models ('bloody instructions').[27] Such a shutting out, in principle, of the very idea that 'developing' countries might have anything at all to contribute to the nature and direction of enterprise only accelerates the drift towards a downward spiral of dependency – of disembedded, culturally alienating and ecologically destructive, unsustainable development. Proof of this cultural blindness, if proof were needed, is the fact that such business and enterprise pedagogy is not only virtually devoid of contributions by women – a serious drawback by any standard – but by Third World thinkers and practitioners as well.

Yet, Third World theories and methods of management which allow 'developing' populations to become economically literate inside complex production processes and thus enable them to reverse the marginalisation to which their enforced displacement has reduced them, do exist.[28] Such frameworks which nurture, rather than exploit, the obliterated, the dominated, the expendables, the displaced, the landless, those trying to survive in today's world of a 'capitalism-of-poverty', remain unknown, unresearched and undocumented. There are, first of all, the autonomous enterprise spaces of the *informal sector* of the economy, which, notwithstanding the onslaught by foreign and alienating enterprise models, continue to survive. These can serve as models of a re-invigoration of local enterprise culture in other spaces and can become part of a culture of resistance to the indoctrination of and acculturation to maldevelopment.

Hassan Zaoual, a Moroccan social economist, gives one such example, where he describes the culturally-embedded 'grocery model' of local enterprise culture among the Soussi, a Berber tribe, in Morocco.[29] The Soussis' business acumen relies on a multiplicity of trading funds circulating within a network of solidarity and accumulation. The enterprise culture of which they partake is a direct result of a synthesis between tradition(s) which are nurtured and sustained by local 'symbolic systems'.[30] The clan spirit operates as economic motor and produces some rather surprising effects, such as the phenomenon of 'private collective property', a rich form of economic cultural diversity, utterly unknown, or lost, in the standardised, ultra-competitive and ultimately impoverished Western version of enterprise. There is, also, the 'Tontine' economy, an example of the 'relational economy' countermodel to the Western insulary 'rational economy' model. Tontines are culturally-embedded savings co-ops rooted in social relations,[31] enduring, living examples of what is possible and feasible in the realm of popular economics and enterprise.[32] In Britain and other post-industrial societies we have the example of 'LETS' (Local Exchange Trading Systems), which are community-owned approaches to business and enterprise. They could, financial commentators already admit, 'easily sidestep the main economy and make the current public-ownership debate irrelevant'.[33] *Seikatsu* – (Japan's family-based consumer cooperative networks owned primarily by women) – and Community Supported Agricultural Schemes in America and Britain, show how a direct relationship between the producer and the buyer/user can benefit both parties, as well as ensuring ecological standards that are respected and constantly improved.[34] The Fair Trade movement seeks to ensure justice in international trading by linking networks of producers and consumers in North and South, sometimes with the support of their local authorities and public servants, thereby achieving a combination of social equity and environmental protection in economic development.[35]

OWNERSHIP AND CONTROL: THE QUESTION IGNORED BY BUSINESS ETHICS

These diverse cultural models share in common the fact that they owe their vigour to the regenerative power of culture and the creative inventiveness of citizens' agency. They are founded on an innate respect for human need and ecological limits, and are embedded in cultures that value cooperative production and collective ownership. In our struggle for sustainability, North and South have much to learn from each other, the former perhaps a bit more from the latter. Mainstream business remains the major shaper and instrument of unsustainable development. Given this, the question of who owns and controls what kind of business is fast becoming the essential question for business ethics to ask. In the end, everything hinges on our ability to re-appreciate our values and priorities, reject the 'economic myth',[36] and take on again the task of re-inventing a future sustainable social and natural environment.

NOTES

1 Esteva, Gustavo (1992) 'Development'; in Sachs, W. (ed.), *The Development Dictionary*, London: ZED Books, p. 6.

2 Shiva, Vandana (1989) *Staying Alive: women, ecology and development*, London: ZED Books.

3 Röben, Bärbel (1994) 'The North must Develop Itself: What would Alternative Prosperity Models look like?', *Development and Cooperation*, July/Aug, 4, p. 16.

4 Sachs, Wolfgang (1995), in *Jajarkot Permaculture Newsletter & Progress* Nepal, p. 2.

5 For example, see Meadows *et al.* (1992) *Beyond the Limits – Global Collapse or a Sustainable Future*, London: Earthscan.

6 ICC (1989), in *Development, Journal of SID*, 2(2), p. 37.

7 BCSD (1992) Cambridge, Mass: MIT Press.

8 Meadows, D. and Meadows, D. (1972) *The Limits to Growth: a report of the Club of Rome*, New York: Universe Books.

9 Group of Lisbon (Petrella, Riccardo) (1995) *Limits to Competition*, Cambridge, Mass.: MIT Press.

10 Petrella, Riccardo (1991) *L'Évangile de la Compétitivité: malheur aux faibles et aux exclus* (The gospel of competition: woe unto the weak and the excluded), in *Le Monde Diplomatique*, Paris: Sept.

11 Hill, C. *et al.* (1994) *Benefiting Business and the Environment: Case Studies of Cost Savings and New Opportunities from Environmental Initiatives*, London: IBE.

12 Hawken, Paul (1993) *The Ecology of Commerce: How Business can save the Planet*, London: Weidenfield & Nicolson, p. viii.

13 Henricks, R. (1990) *Lao Tzu – Te Tao Ching* (trans.), London: The Bodley Head.
14 See Galeano, Eduardo (1973) *Open Veins of Latin America. Five Centuries of Pillage of a Continent*, New York: Monthly Review Press; Rodney, Walter (1973) *How Europe Underdeveloped Africa*, Bogle l'Ouverture; Brown, Michael Barratt (1993) *Fair Trade – Reform and Realities in the International Trading System*, London: ZED Books.
15 Rojas, J. (1994) 'UNCED: Ethics and Development from the Indigenous Point of View', in Brown, N. and Quiblier, P. (eds), *Ethics and Agenda 21*, UNEP, p. 50.
16 Middleton, N., O'Keeffe, P. H. and Moyo, S. (1994) *The Tears of the Crocodile: From Rio to Reality in the Developing World*, London: Pluto Press.
17 Röben, 'The North must Develop Itself'.
18 For example, see Max-Neef, Manfred (1991) *How Much is Enough? Max-Neef in conversation with Satish Kumar*, Schumacher College: *The Schumacher Series*, London: Phil Shepherd Productions; see also Stead, W. E. and Stead, J. G. (1994) 'Can Humankind Change the Economic Myth? Paradigm shifts are necessary for ecologically sustainable business', *Journal of Organizational Change Management*, 7(4), pp. 15–31.
19 Max-Neef, *How Much is Enough?*.
20 Daly, Herman and Cobb, John (1990) *For the Common Good*, London: Green Print.
21 Rahman, Anisur (1993) *People's Self-Development*, London: ZED Books; see also Hawken, *The Ecology of Commerce*.
22 Daly and Cobb, *For the Common Good*, p. 138.
23 Carmen, Raff E. (in press) *Autonomous Development: The Humanisation of the Landscape*, London: ZED Books.
24 Interview with Riccardo Petrella, Lisbon Group Founder, 'Politics has abdicated in favour of Private Enterprise', in *The Courier*, EU, Brussels, No. 115, May–June 1995, p. 4.
25 Middleton *et al.*, *The Tears of the Crocodile*.
26 Villier, Gauthier (1992) *Le Pauvre, le Hors-la-Loi et le Métis* (The Poor, the Outlaw and the Métis), Brussels: CEDAF-ASDOC Cahier, No. 6.
27 Davies, Peter W. F and Lubelski, Marek (1995) *Ethics, Literacy and the Business of Management Education*, paper presented to the University of Leeds conference on 'New Perspectives on Management Education', 12–13 January 1995.
28 Carmen, Raff E. (1995) '*Clodomir Santos de Morais*; Workshop for Enterprise Management (WEM) v. "British" Enterprise Training: the difference is in the context', *Convergence*, Toronto, XVII(1), p. 72.
29 Zaoual, Hassan (1994) 'La Culture: Etage du Développement' (Culture, the Hostage of Development), in *Cultures and Development*, Brussels, 16/17.
30 An alternative to the much-abused word 'culture'.
31 Hence 'relational' economy.
32 Sizoo, Edith (1991) 'Les Tontines à Enchères au Cameroon' (Tontines

by Auction in Cameroon – an example of popular economics), in *Cultures and Development*, Brussels, 5/6.

33 Cowe, Roger (1995) 'Solutions that lie with people: Let's get together', *Guardian*, 25 April, p. 13.

34 Plant, C. and Plant, J. (eds) (1991) *Green Business – Hope or Hoax*, Dartington, Totnes, Devon: Green Books.

35 Brown, *Fair Trade*.

36 Stead and Stead, *Can Humankind Change the Economic Myth?*

3

CORPORATE GOVERNANCE AND ETHICS

Philip Stiles

INTRODUCTION

The general heading of business ethics covers a large field, ranging from broad topics such as the meaning and role of business activity (usually presented as a critique of capitalism), to narrower issues such as the individual moral dilemmas faced by managers. But between the broad and the narrow lie issues concerning the management of the corporation as a unit.[1] Within this middle ground the debate on corporate governance is conducted, a debate which is chiefly concerned with examining the power and accountability of organisations and, more particularly, the roles and responsibilities of boards of directors.

The increased interest in corporate governance has mirrored the rise in concern in business ethics generally, with the voluminous literature on high profile scandals and failures in firms providing a common base for much descriptive and prescriptive work in both areas. Both subjects, too, share a key focus on agency problems, which has driven much theoretical and empirical work. Many commentators on corporate governance assume that boards, if properly harnessed, can bring important performance gains. Many ethical theorists share a parallel assumption about the bottom-line benefits of utilising ethical management principles.

The aim of this chapter is to examine some of the key issues within corporate governance, and to identify some of the important ethical implications arising from them. The nature of this chapter will be a broad review of themes from the various strands of the corporate governance debate, highlighting the ethical issues these generate. In terms of structure, the two key relationships, (i) between the board and shareholders, and (ii) between the board and shareholders and society, will be examined, and a concluding section will discuss the merits (or demerits) of self-regulation as a means of improving corporate governance practice.

KEY ISSUES IN CORPORATE GOVERNANCE

Corporate governance is defined as the system by which companies are directed and controlled. The unit of analysis is generally the board of directors, who are 'responsible for the governance of their companies',[2] but it is generally recognised that the board is only one mechanism in the governance of organisations, a point we shall return to later. There has been an intense focus on the activities of boards following a series of well-publicised corporate scandals and failures. Issues of ethical concern which have emerged are excessive CEO (chief executive officer) power (Maxwell), fraud (BCCI), insider trading (the Guinness case), the misleading of shareholders (Blue Arrow), executive remuneration (British Gas) and such practices as the milking of pension funds, use of golden parachutes, poison pills and greenmail. Such issues as these have brought a certain cynicism about business conduct in general and may have contributed to a lowering of confidence in the system of monitoring and control of companies.

Sir Adrian Cadbury states that the heart of the matter of governance 'is how to achieve a balance between the essential power of companies and their proper accountability'.[3] According to Monks and Minow,[4] accountability consists of two relationships, first, the accountability of boards to shareholders and, second, the accountability of both to society. It is the first relationship which has dominated the corporate governance literature, and we shall turn our attention to this area first.

Boards and shareholders

Shareholders appoint the directors of a company, and all directors are legally obliged to act in the interests of shareholders. Directors have a number of duties to the company – primarily, a duty of care, a fiduciary duty and a duty to act within one's powers within the capacity of the company. The board must, as a minimum, fulfil its legal requirements,[5] but there is a great deal of latitude in the extent to which a board can get involved in the running of a company. This can best be represented as a continuum with, at one end, a pas-

sive board, largely ceremonial in function, restricted to ru
stamping the decisions and policies of management, and, at the
other end, a highly proactive board, involved in strategic decision-
making and vigorous in monitoring the actions of management and
ensuring the company acts in the best interests of shareholders.
Where a board sits on this continuum will depend largely on company size and type, industry category, stage in company lifecycle,
whether it is in stable or crisis conditions and, of course, on the
composition of the board, the characteristics of the directors, and
the locus of power between directors and management.[6]

From the theoretical literature, boards of directors can be viewed
as a mechanism for harmonising agency conflicts and safeguarding
invested capital, an instrument of control by which managers control other managers, a 'cooptative' mechanism for a company to
link itself with the external environment to secure resources and, on
occasion, to protect itself against environmental adversity, and a
mechanism to perpetuate this ruling elite and encourage the
strengthening of it through interlocking directorates. A typical list
of board roles and responsibilities is as follows:

1 Formulating strategy
2 Developing policy
3 Supervising executive management
4 Maintaining accountability

On most views of board endeavour, strategic planning and decision-making are considered to be the principal functions. Though
empirical evidence to support this claim is sparse, there is general
consensus that board involvement in these areas contributes to
more effective performance on the part of the company.[7] The
board's involvement in strategy brings directors sharply into the
ethical spotlight. Decisions on strategic issues are inevitably value
laden and, as Pettigrew states: 'all strategies can be assessed or
interpreted in a way that links them to an apparent ethical framework'.[8] To take a simple example, the decision of an engineering
company to bid for military contracts represents a strategic decision
which has significant ethical overtones. Even where managerial control is significant, boards still determine the boundaries of strategic
decision-making.[9] Boards also set the ethical tone with regard to
their monitoring and accountability roles. What is expected of management, both by way of performance and behaviour, is ultimately
the responsibility of the directors.[10]

The board is thus recognised as being crucial in the process of developing an ethical framework, implicit or explicit, for the formulation of strategy and policy, monitoring management and ensuring accountability.[11] A common manifestation of board leadership in this role is the production of corporate codes of ethics, which are intended to capture succinctly the guiding principles of the organisation. The efficacy of such codes, and the problem of how their values are communicated and enforced, are important issues, but we shall not address ourselves to those here. The important point is that, for a board to be effective, it should play a significant role in running the company.[12]

However, the effectiveness of the board of directors as a concept has been called into question. The managerial hegemony theory describes the board as holding nominal but not real power within the organisation. The real responsibility of running and controlling the company, according to this theory, is assumed by corporate management. Boards, on this view, are often considered to be 'the creatures of the CEO'.[13] The role of the board, therefore, is limited by the domination of management, and particularly of the CEO, who designs and leads the board and controls the flow of information to directors. As a result, the board is passive, and has no input into organisational decision-making. Nor does it exercise control over the performance of the chief executive or the company as a whole, which, in the eyes of shareholders, makes the board ineffective. The board of directors is thus presented as a legal fiction, dominated by management, making it ineffective in reducing the potential for agency problems between management and shareholders. The board's role in representing the conscience of the company is also constrained by managerial domination.

The ethical issues which arise from such a view are considerable. The inability of boards to harmonise agency conflicts and safeguard invested capital can be seen in the widespread reports of corporate malfeasance, excessive managerial remuneration and the abuse of managerial perks. Managers have also been recorded as pursuing diversification strategies in order to increase firm size and, with it, associated prestige for themselves as individuals.[14]

There has been a range of proposals to address these concerns, covering both the structure of boards and the role of shareholders. The key proposals for board structure are to split the roles of chairman and chief executive, to have sufficient numbers of independent non-executive directors on the board, and by introducing audit and remuneration committees. The object has been to build 'contestabil-ity' in the boardroom,[15] with power not residing in the hands of one individual; with non-executives monitoring the performance and conduct of executives and asking discerning questions; and with the use of board committees encouraging greater democracy and accountability and freeing up main board time for other key issues.

These ideas for change in UK (and US) corporate governance practice have taken place in the context of a clear consensus for pre-serving the unitary board. Though there has been an insistence on a clear separation between executive and non-executive directors, and even calls for shareholders committees, the move towards German-style two-tier boards has been fiercely resisted. Indeed, the Cadbury Report has been heavily criticised as attempting to bring in two-tier boards 'by the back door'. This criticism centres on the interpreta-tion of the non-executives' role as 'policemen', overseeing the per-formance of the executives and, because of their objective status, acting as guardians of the moral probity of the firm. However, a number of problems beset the non-executives' position. First, liabil-ity extends to all directors, not just the executives, so there may be reluctance on the part of non-executives to reveal the true extent of any malfeasance. Second, non-executives are still largely chosen by the chief executive of the company, which may make the non-execu-tive less likely to ask tough questions of the CEO. Third, their lack of specific knowledge of the organisation means they must rely to a great extent on the integrity of executives to provide them with accurate information. Fourth, there is a paradox inherent in the role of the non-executive, a paradox neatly brought out by Demb and Neubauer.[16] A non-executive, to be effective, should become involved in the organisation and have a good understanding of the business in order to make informed contributions at board meet-ings. However, the more involved in the company the non-executive becomes, the greater the danger that his/her independence will decrease, as he/she identifies more closely with the organisation and its executives.

Scepticism about the role of the board in ensuring corporate accountability, and a loss of faith in accounting and auditing prac-tices, have brought calls for greater shareholder intervention in the running of organisations. This has provoked a fierce debate and a polarisation of opinion.[17] One view states that shareholders should maximise their own economic self-interest and not become involved in issues of corporate governance. If shareholders are unhappy with a firm's managers, they can simply walk away and the predictable fall in the firm's share price will put pressure on incumbent managers. Shareholders who adopt this approach have been pejoratively named 'punter-capitalists', or accused of having a 'betting-slip mentality'.[18] The opposing view is for greater shareholder involvement. Strengthening the role of shareholders has been a popular refrain in calls for reform in corporate governance,[19] and there are signs that this trend is becoming increasingly important. In 1993, directors at Kodak, IBM and Westinghouse were ousted from their boards due to shareholder pressure.[20] The rise of shareholder activism has come about as a result of well publicised cases of management who were distinctly unaccountable, of a weakening belief in the efficient market theory, and of the fact that major shareholders who owned large chunks of underperforming or mismanaged businesses could not sell stock easily, unless by providing a substantial discount.[21] Scepticism about the traditional mechanisms of corporate accountability, primarily the board (and particularly the effectiveness of non-executive directors), controversies surrounding executive remuneration, and a loss of faith in accounting and auditing practices, have added strength to the case for shareholder intervention. The growth of institutional investors, particularly the pension funds, makes greater intervention possible.[22]

In summary, boards are seen as key mechanisms for controlling the conduct and performance of organisations in order to protect the interests of shareholders. Involvement in strategy and ensuring effective monitoring of the firm inevitably raise ethical issues over the choice of strategy, how it is implemented, the nature of the goals set for employees, and how their performance is monitored and evaluated. In short, the board, as the apex of the company, should set the ethical framework within which it operates. But the effectiveness of boards as instruments for ensuring managerial accountability to shareholders has been called into question. Demands for shareholders to become more involved in monitoring companies and improving standards of corporate behaviour have received a variable reception. But what of the wider responsibilities of the firm? In the next section, we shall examine the relationship of the board and the shareholders with society.

Boards and shareholders: their relationship to society

The relationship of boards and shareholders to society has usually been examined within the corporate social responsibility literature. This literature is extensive, and consists largely of databased surveys, representing corporate virtue in the light of the contents of annual reports, codes of conduct, reputation, philanthropy or environmentalism.[23] However, the field has been beset by definitional problems and a diversity of approach has put serious limitations on theory-building.

A more promising area has been the development of stakeholder theory. It is revealing that, though boards of directors have been studied using a number of theoretical lenses, notably agency theory, resource dependency theory, stewardship theory and class hegemony theory, there has been little work undertaken in the area of stakeholder theory, and few empirical studies exist which examine the relationship between boards of directors and their stakeholder orientations.[24] As a consequence, the board's activity with regard to corporate social performance is certainly an under-researched area.

Stakeholder analysis has been called the *sine qua non* of business virtue.[25] The recognition that organisations should move from a shareholder to a stakeholder perspective is the central tenet of stakeholder theory. A stakeholder is defined as 'any group or individual who can affect or is affected by the achievement of the firm's objectives'.[26] These stakeholders include owners, consumer advocates, customers, competitors, media, employees, environmentalists, suppliers, governments, and local community organisations. These groups or individuals all have, according to the theory, a legitimate stake in the organisation and are in a position to affect organisational outcomes. There has been disagreement over who should be included among the stakeholders and whether it is sensible to assign priorities to certain groups, but the central idea is clear.

The problems for stakeholder theory are several. First, the decision-making process may become lengthy if all competing claims of stakeholders have to be considered. Second, there seems to be no clear decision-rule when attempting to adjudicate between rival claims of stakeholders.[27] Third, how are bosses to be judged if they are accountable to many stakeholders? Fourth, if other stakeholders are put before shareholders, this may reduce share values and may bring less willingness to invest.[28] The lack of research on how decisions at board level are taken when a stakeholder orientation is adopted has further limited the acceptance of the model.

However, there is a growing realisation on the part of many commentators that the responsibilities of the board should not be limited solely to concern for shareholders' interests. Part of this shift has to do with concerns about corporate legitimacy. Dahl's assertion that 'every large corporation should be thought of as a social enterprise, that is, as an entity whose existence and decisions can be justified only insofar as they serve public or social purposes'[29] is cited approvingly by Parkinson in his seminal work on corporate power. Many boards now speak of balancing the interests of various interested groups and, at the level of the community as a whole, Parkinson notes that:

> Whatever the precise significance of the profit motive it is clear that the level of social activism increased significantly in the 1980s and has largely been sustained since. The last decade has also been marked by a growth in bodies whose whole aim is to promote social activism, such as Business in the Community, the Per Cent Club, and the Action Resource Centre.[30]

Hosmer[31] argues that trust, commitment and effort on the part of all stakeholders of a firm are essential to competitive success, because an *integrity of common purpose* will produce co-operative actions and help the innovation process'.

In the UK, most decisions made by companies concerning external groups with legitimate interests in the organisation are made without those external constituencies being part of the decision-making process itself. Because stakeholders typically do not take part in corporate decision-making, they suffer from a disadvantage in terms of the information about the company, its practices and the impact of its policies. Third-party monitoring of corporate performance is also difficult, primarily for this reason. Several reforms have been suggested to increase the position of stakeholders and ensure better social responsibility on the part of companies. Two recurring calls are for mandatory disclosure of information, and for increasing stakeholder representation within the company (for example, by instituting works councils). Such calls have met with resistance, but companies have realised that greater awareness of external interests does bring benefits, and not only in terms of favourable PR. A major driver in the move towards increased social responsibility is the avoidance of the imposition of regulation or legislation.

SELF-REGULATION OR LEGISLATION?

A central question in the corporate governance debate concerns whether organisations can effectively regulate themselves and whether reform should be introduced in the form of standards, codes, regulations, or whether legislation is required. In terms of the UK, Prentice[32] states that 'government is very much a spectator, content to leave it to the City to sort out its own problems'. Certainly, the government believes that self-regulation is the best approach for ensuring good corporate governance, for a number of reasons. First, it is thought that, though legislation might encourage better behaviour, it cannot ensure it. Second, a totally prescriptive approach might stifle the creativity of entrepreneurs. Third, legislative change can be a very slow process, whereas in comparison, self-regulatory change is almost immediate and so is more effective. The Cadbury Report strongly advocated maintaining the present system of self-regulation. Many corporate boards, in addition to adhering to the Cadbury recommendations, have responded to the increased focus on organisational behaviour and accountability by establishing (or updating) codes of ethics. Other professional bodies have also produced new codes of conduct, and ethics committees have been set up in an increasing number of corporations.

There is the criticism that such standards or codes are adopted by precisely the companies which do not need them – the well-run organisations who already have sound principles. Such critics argue: what would it take to stop a Maxwell? The call for greater legislation is predictable, and the tightening up of pension law which resulted from the Maxwell case has been a strong benefit. But it is difficult to see what could have prevented Maxwell's fraud. No system of regulation is complete. But as Neil Hamilton, then UK Minister for Corporate Affairs, said at a conference on corporate governance:

> We (the government) think the system of self-regulation to be a workable one. But if there are more scandals, more breaches of law, then we shall have to think of introducing more legislation.[33]

CONCLUSION

The conduct of companies, and the systems by which they are controlled and regulated, are central areas of investigation for business ethics. The actions of companies, particularly public corporations, can have large consequences, making the concepts of responsibility and accountability crucially important. We have seen in broad outline that the relationship between the board and the shareholders leads to a number of structural problems. Managerial domination of boards leads to agency issues which generate a plethora of ethical concerns. In terms of the relationship between organisations and society, there appears to be growing recognition of the importance of stakeholders (though again this is not without its problems). Calls for reform of boards and of systems of corporate governance in general persist, but as the case of Maxwell shows, it is extremely difficult to stop rogue entrepreneurs disregarding their responsibilities. Effective corporate governance ultimately rests on the quality and integrity of organisations and their employees.

NOTES

1 Goodpaster, K. and Matthews, J. B. (1982) 'Can a Corporation Have a Conscience?' *Harvard Business Review*, 60(1), pp. 132–41.

2 Cadbury Committee (1992) *Report on the Financial Aspects of Corporate Governance*, London: Gee Publishing.

3 Cadbury, Sir A. (1993) 'Review of Monks and Minow's Power and Accountability', *Corporate Governance: An International Review*, 1(2), p. 60.

4 Monks, R. A. G. and Minow, N. (1991) *Power and Accountability*, New York: HarperCollins.

5 Mace, M. L. (1971) *Directors: Myth and Reality*, Boston: Harvard University Press.

6 Dulewicz, S. V. D., Herbert, P. J. A. H. and Stiles, P. (1995) *Standards of Good Practice for Boards of Directors*, London: Institute of Directors with Henley Management College.

7 For example, see Zahra, S. A and Pearce, J. (1989) 'Boards of Directors and Corporate Performance: A Review and Integrative Model', *Journal of Management*, 15(2), pp. 291–334; and Demb, A. and Neubauer F. F. (1992) *The Corporate Board: Confronting the Paradoxes*, Oxford: Oxford University Press.

8 Pettigrew, M. A. (1992) *Boards of Directors: A Review of Recent Literature*, Warwick: Warwick Business School Centre for Corporate Strategy and Change.

9 Mizruchi, M. S. (1983) 'Who Controls Whom? An Examination of the Relation between Management and Boards of Directors in large

American Corporations', *Academy of Management Review*, 8, pp. 426–35.

10 Pettigrew, *Boards of Directors*.

11 Andrews, K. A. (1989) 'Ethics in Practice', *Harvard Business Review*, September–October, 67(5), pp. 99–104.

12 Pettigrew, *Boards of Directors*.

13 Mace, *Directors: Myth and Reality*.

14 Jensen, M. and Meckling, W. (1976) 'Theory of the Firm, Managerial Behaviour, Agency Costs and Ownership Structure', *Journal of Financial Economics*, 3, pp. 305–60.

15 *Economist* (1994) *Watching the Boss: A Survey of Corporate Governance*, 29 January.

16 Demb and Neubauer, *The Corporate Board*.

17 Prentice, D. D. (1993) 'Some Aspects of the Corporate Governance Debate', in Prentice, D. D and Holland, P. R. J. (eds), *Contemporary Issues in Corporate Governance*, Oxford University Press, pp. 25–44.

18 Prentice, 'Some Aspects of the Corporate Governance Debate'.

19 Monks and Minow, *Power and Accountability*; see also Nader, R. (1984) 'Reforming Corporate Governance', *California Management Review*, 26(4), pp. 126–32.

20 *Economist, Watching the Boss*.

21 *Economist, Watching the Boss*.

22 Davies, P. (1993) 'Institutional Investors in the United Kingdom', in Prentice and Holland, *Contemporary Issues in Corporate Governance*, pp. 69–96.

23 Nicholson, N. (1994) 'Ethics in Organisations: A Framework for Theory and Research', *Journal of Business Ethics*, 13(8), pp. 581–96.

24 Wang, J. and Dewhirst, H. D. (1992) 'Boards of Directors and Stakeholder Orientation', *Journal of Business Ethics*, 11(2), pp. 115–23.

25 O'Toole, J. (1991) 'Do Good, Do Well; The Business Enterprise Trust Awards', *California Management Review*, 53(3), pp. 9–24.

26 Freeman, R. E. (1984) *Strategic Management: A Stakeholder Approach*, Boston: Ballinger.

27 Mahoney, J. (1994) 'What Makes a Business Company Ethical?', *Business Strategy Review*, 5(4), Winter, pp. 1–16.

28 *Economist, Watching the Boss*.

29 Quoted in Pettigrew, *Boards of Directors*.

30 Parkinson, J. E. (1994) *Corporate Power and Responsibility*, Oxford: Oxford University Press, p. 297.

31 Hosmer, Larue T. (1994) 'Strategic Planning as if Ethics Mattered', *Strategic Management Journal*, 15, pp. 17–34.

32 Prentice, 'Some Aspects of the Corporate Governance Debate'.

33 Hamilton, N. (1992) *Corporate Governance*, paper given at a conference of the Strategic Management Society, London.

4

BUSINESS AND ITS SOCIAL RESPONSIBILITY

Andrew Wilson

INTRODUCTION

In recent years there has been an emerging consensus among business leaders – in small and large organisations alike – that the role and responsibility of business extends well beyond the critical importance of wealth creation. Today, there is widespread acceptance of the view that, if business is to prosper, the environment in which it operates must prosper too. This view was reinforced with the recent publication of the Royal Society of Art's 'Tomorrow's Company' report[1] – a business-led inquiry aimed at identifying sources of sustainable success. One of the report's key messages was that a profitable business sector is vital to funding 'the standard of living and quality of life to which society aspires'. The report calls for an 'inclusive approach' to business, one in which companies see themselves 'as part of a wider system'.

Implicit within this inclusive approach is the concept of an organisation's 'licence to operate'. This licence is granted by all the firm's stakeholders – its shareholders, employees, customers, suppliers, the local community, and any number of pressure groups. Not only do all these different stakeholders have an interest in the activities of business, it is becoming increasingly clear that, in many instances, they have the potential to influence the way in which business conducts itself. If business does not retain the approval and support of the majority of its stakeholders, it jeopardises its trading position.

It is important to recognise that the concept of a firm's licence to operate is far more than a manifestation of customer loyalty or brand affiliation (although consumers do have leverage in this direction). It concerns individuals, acting alone or collectively, who seek

50

to shape and influence the relationship between business and society. How, then, are these forces impacting upon business, and what pressures will the responsible company need to respond to if it is to retain its licence to operate in the coming years?

DISCERNING CUSTOMERS

The recent rapid rise in the green movement, and the publication of such journals as the *New Consumer Magazine*, are contributing pressures to an increasingly competitive marketplace for a whole range of consumer goods and services. Manufacturers and service providers can no longer ignore the environmental impact of their activities. It would seem that consumers are becoming increasingly vociferous in their reactions to business behaviour. The demonstrations across Europe in the Summer of 1995 against Shell UK's plans to dump the Brent Spar oil storage platform at sea, and the subsequent reversal of those plans, are simply one of the most recent manifestations of this trend.

Research by the Chartered Institute of Marketing[2] has shown that, despite the recession, consumer attitudes towards issues of social responsibility have hardened. So, for example, 64 per cent of consumers questioned said that a company's record in environmental matters and social behaviour influences their purchasing decisions, compared with only 51 per cent in 1981.

In addition, customers are also expressing ethical concerns about the products and service available to them. Research by Mintel[3] reveals a marked rise in consumer awareness about the ethical dimension of business. Almost half of those surveyed (47 per cent) said they would not use any financial service (bank or building society account, credit card or investment) from an organisation they felt to be ethically unsound.

The Ethical Consumer Research Association publishes a consumer guide which advises shoppers on the ethical track record of firms which produce a wide range of household products. In addition, the book 'Changing Corporate Values'[4] informs readers of an organisation's track record in such issues as disclosure of information, employment issues including pay and conditions, industrial democracy, equal opportunities, community involvement and respect for people. If purchasing decisions are to be influenced by such factors, then it is clear that the responsible company needs to ensure that its behaviour in these areas can withstand close scrutiny.

Indeed, many organisations are already awake to this fact. The Cooperative Bank, for example, were keen to relate recent increases in the number of new retail deposits to their marketing campaign which underlines their ethical investment policy. The company announced that it would not be involved with tobacco companies, those with a poor environmental record, or those involved with factory farming and animal testing. As a result the bank saw an increase in new customers of 13 per cent, largely among white-collar managerial employees in the 25 to 40 age group.

The whole movement towards ethical consumerism is fuelled by higher real incomes and a greater awareness of the issues involved. However, it is fair to question whether this is a short-term fad or an irreversible social trend. On the one hand, there is evidence to suggest that consumers are willing to act on their values with conviction. Research by Mintel,[5] for example, has shown that a majority of consumers are prepared to pay a premium of between 8 and 13 per cent for 'environmentally friendly/ethical' foods and toiletries. On the other hand, there are those who claim that consumers still lack sufficiently detailed information about companies to make informed judgements about their activities. In addition, there have been several well-publicised examples of corporate malpractice recently that have had little or no impact on customer behaviour. In some circumstances, consumers retain little or no choice in whom they do business with.

DISCERNING JOBSEEKERS

The recent past has seen the emergence of the principled jobseeker.[6] Potential employees, and most especially young graduates, are asking searching questions about how prospective employers conduct their business. Objections to working in certain sectors, such as the nuclear or defence industries, are being overtaken by a more general desire to work for a company that is both seen to be behaving in a responsible manner and is returning something to the community in which it operates.

With graduate unemployment at its highest rate for many years, most employers are untroubled by recruitment difficulties in this sector of the labour market. However, the demographic pressures that caused the tight labour market conditions characteristic of the late 1980s have not gone away. The dramatic fall in the number of young people able to enter the labour market is only gradually beginning to turn around. It is likely that economic recovery will once again see the young, skilled jobseeker in great demand. When this happens, employers who have a well publicised ethical and community-focused stance are likely to benefit by their ability to attract the best available people.

Research carried out among recent graduates[7] reveals that the business leaders of tomorrow have very clear ideas about corporate responsibilities. When considering potential employers, business students rated a good corporate reputation as the second most important factor, ahead of starting salary or fringe benefits. What criteria did they use to define corporate reputation? The three most important issues were: providing quality services; expanding into new markets; and being a good corporate citizen, caring about the community and the environment.

Once again, there are concrete examples of companies already taking action in this area. Whitbread ran a successful recruitment campaign aimed specifically at graduates which highlighted the work the company carries out in the community, working with voluntary sector, charitable and not-for-profit organisations. In addition, Marks & Spencer (regarded by many as one of the top graduate management trainers in the country) recently announced that it is to offer graduates a programme of one year's work experience. This scheme is being put forward as a philanthropic act to help graduates to find employment, but it is one that clearly has benefits for the company's reputation.

DISCERNING INVESTORS

The concept of ethical investment is far from new, and in recent years its popularity among both institutional investors and the public has grown rapidly. There are now vast sums of money invested according to ethical criteria each year. Estimates suggests that the charitable sector alone – which is generally associated with ethical investment – has more than £20 billion under investment.[8] Other figures, compiled by investment advisers PIRC, suggest that as much as £100 billion is invested in Britain with some sort of social objective in mind.

Ethical investors, and the organisations which serve them, analyse potential investment opportunities against a wide range of criteria. For example, people choose not to invest in companies that deal with tobacco products, alcohol or gambling; that have a poor environmental or ecological record; that trade with countries that do not respect human rights; or that are involved in arms production. Increasingly, however, people are widening their tests of acceptability to include the ethical behaviour of businesses.[9]

There is growing evidence to suggest that there are widely divergent views about the popularity of ethical investment between those inside companies and investors outside organisations. According to one recent report[10] only 7 per cent of businesses sampled believed shareholders were more likely to invest in companies which work with charities. In contrast, 78 per cent of shareholders stated that they would rather invest in a company that works with charity. Further research by MORI[11] found that 59 per cent of institutional investors polled held more favourable impressions of companies that contribute to the local community in which they operate. In contrast, only 4 per cent of these investors looked less favourably upon such companies.

Indeed, developments in this field are moving at such a pace that several organisations are urging British investors to follow the American route and start buying shares in companies with poor working practices and unethical trading records.[12] The idea is that shareholders should militate for reform from within the company, using their rights as part-owners of the company to raise with the board issues that are of concern to them as individuals.

Despite these trends, many commentators raise doubts about the level of real choice available to investors. While individuals might prefer to invest their funds ethically, most share ownership is controlled by institutional investors, who have less freedom. The law in Britain forces the managers of pension funds, for example, to operate under fairly tight restrictions. In addition, there is still a great deal of confusion and controversy in this relatively new area of the financial markets. How many of the investors in Eagle Star's Environmental Opportunities unit trust, for example, are aware that Eagle Star is a subsidiary of British American Tobacco?

DISCERNING EMPLOYEES

Many companies are seeking to encourage a greater degree of innovation and entrepreneurship in their workforce. Autocratic management styles are being replaced with teamwork, leadership and empowerment. Typically, managers are heard to say such things as, 'you can't tell people any more, you have to convince them', or 'I have to influence my people rather than organise them'. The movement towards flatter corporate structures, the devolution of responsibility, and the increasing emphasis on quality, all go hand-in-hand with a greater need to ensure that workers have a clear sense of what the company stands for. This implies that companies need to articulate the values inherent at the heart of the organisation and to ensure the mechanisms are in place to translate these values into actions.

In parallel with these trends, the removal of traditional command and control structures, as business seeks to empower employees, means that organisations are seeking alternative ways to encourage motivation and dedication from their workforce. However, the evidence suggests that most firms have a long way to go in this respect. A recent survey carried out for the Department of Employment[13] shows that only a minority of the sample of almost 3500 working men and women questioned felt strongly committed to their employers. Less than one third said they would turn down an offer of a better-paid job to stay with their current organisation. This said, pay is far from the only, or indeed the most important, factor in determining attitudes towards employment.

For example, the same survey found that two-thirds of respondents would still want to carry on working even if they were financially independent. Other research on attitudes to work by the Henley Centre suggests that, for most people, the social needs for work now have a greater importance than economic needs. This was confirmed by research carried out by IRS, who found that the amount earned came fourth in a list of priorities, behind fairness and respect, challenging work, and freedom to get the job done.

Hence, companies need to look more carefully at the congruence between their own values and those of individual employees if they are to retain a loyal and committed workforce. This message was strongly reinforced by recent research carried out by the Ashridge Management Research Group among a sample of senior managers.[14] Less than one in five managers feel that their current employer displays the attributes of their ideal organisation. One of the key factors influencing management commitment is an organisation that demonstrates behaviour congruent with a well-defined value statement. In particular, managers seek a company that truly lives up to the maxim that 'people are our most important asset'.

For some companies, most notably those in the United States, this process is so well advanced it has become second nature. One such example is that of the ice cream manufacturer Ben and Jerry's. This company, with an annual turnover of $100 million, employs a workforce of some 400 people. Its values are enshrined in a mission statement that talks of the company's product mission, its social mission, and its economic mission. What makes this company noteworthy is the way in which the values espoused by the mission statement are translated into actions.

Communications are an important aspect to this, with bi-monthly staff meetings, bi-annual employee opinion surveys and annual appraisals that are conducted upwards through the organisation as well as down. In addition, the company has a compensation philosophy which ensures that the ratio between lowest and highest salaries does not exceed 7:1. It also has a profit-sharing plan and a children's centre that is available to the children of both employees and non-workers alike.

Social responsibility within the company extends beyond a programme of corporate community involvement to include a carefully managed system of out-sourcing that ensures supplies are brought from areas around the world that support a philosophy of 'caring capitalism'. For example, cashew and Brazil nuts are purchased from native forest people in Brazil, enabling them to earn income from renewable sources.

Ben and Jerry's is by no means unique – it serves to illustrate how a company can set about ensuring that its employees are fully aware of, involved in and signed-up to the values of the company. In the UK there is ample evidence to suggest that many companies are also taking action in this area. A recent study[15] suggests that almost half of the UK's top 500 companies have enshrined their values in codes of ethics. More than this, however, companies are seriously tackling the issue of not just ensuring employees are aware of codes of ethics, but of generating a real commitment to the values and standards implicit within them. So, for example, organisations are beginning to develop ethics awareness training programmes. They are also installing ethics hot-lines, where employees can both seek confidential advice and assistance on potential grey areas, and report misconduct and unethical practices.

CONCLUDING REMARKS

Milton Friedman has argued that

> there is one and only one social responsibility of business – to use its resources and engage in activities designed to increase its profits so long as it . . . engages in open and free competition without deception or fraud.[16]

Some commentators still support this view and would maintain that the only meaningful measures of a company's worth are its return on capital employed and its earnings per share. However, there is a growing consensus that measures of business success need to embrace the totality of a company's activities.

In this final section, several of the disparate forces outlined above are drawn together in the concept of the social audit, demonstrating how business is attempting to measure many of the less tangible aspects of its wider responsibilities. The importance of developing non-financial measures of corporate performance cannot be overstated. The immediate financial performance of a company is only a partial measure of its success. Only when due weight and credit is given to other aspects of a company's activities will society as a whole begin to redefine the notion of what constitutes good business.

The social audit develops alternative measures that take into account an organisation's relationship with all its stakeholders (employees, customers, suppliers and the community, as well as shareholders). Briefly, it

> examines the social and ethical impact of the business from two perspectives: from the inside – assessing performance against its mission statement or statement of objectives; and from the outside – using comparisons with other organisations' behaviour and social norms.[17]

Contemporary wisdom suggests that, in five or six years time, socially responsible companies will be producing an annual social audit alongside, or incorporated within, its annual financial report. The exact form and nature of the social audit will vary from company to company and it is important not to prescribe exactly what ought, and what ought not, to be included in a social audit. However, there exist today several models of how to create a social audit – one such example is that produced by the organisation Traidcraft.[18]

In essence, the purpose of the social audit is to put some measure to those things that the business does which delivers value to the different stakeholder groups. This might include figures on training, promoting equal opportunities, the composition and salary scales of employees, local economic development, community involvement, allowing staff time for volunteering, reducing the environmental impact of business, or investing in long-term partnership with suppliers.

Currently, if such aspects of business are measured, they are invariably seen as costs rather than investments. For the responsible company, however, efforts spent developing staff, improving community life, bettering the environment or building good relationships with suppliers are all part of a long-term commitment to all its stakeholders groups.

The consequences of ignoring such issues are unlikely to be catastrophic in the short term. However, as the relationship between business and society develops and changes, the importance of corporate social responsibility will grow. This point was made most succinctly by Tom Lloyd in his recent book, *The Nice Company*.

> The nice company will become more dominant not because it is more ethical, but because it is, in the long run, more profitable.[19]

While socially responsible companies might lose ground in the short term to those organisations that indulge in sharp practices, they will undoubtedly reap long-term benefits. More than this, however, unethical organisations will find it becomes increasingly untenable to continue in business. Stakeholder groups are already demonstrating that they are willing to yield their power and influence to shape the impact business has on their lives. The responsible company is well aware of this and is already taking measures to retain its licence to operate.

NOTES

1 RSA (1995) *Tomorrow's Company Inquiry Report*, London: RSA.
2 Chartered Institute of Marketing (1993) *Metamorphosis in Marketing*, London: CIM.
3 Mintel (1994) *The Green Consumer: Vols I and II*, London: Mintel.

4 Adams, R., Carruthers, J. and Hamil, S. (1991) *Changing Corporate Values*, London: Kogan Page.
5 Mintel (1991) *Special Report, Green and Ethical Shopper*, London: Mintel.
6 Charter, M. (ed.) (1992) *Greener Marketing*, Sheffield: Greenleaf; see also Morgan, D. (1990) 'Marketing Your Principles', *The Times*, 26 April.
7 Prince Of Wales Business Leaders Forum (1993) *Corporate Reputation in Tomorrow's Marketplace*, London.
8 *Investors Chronicle, Professional Investment for Charities*, 29 March 1991.
9 Northedge, Richard (1993) 'Ethical Funds to Examine the Dirty-Tricks Factor', *Daily Telegraph*, 18 January.
10 National Children's Home (1992) *In Business With Charities*, London.
11 MORI (1993) *Captains of Industry Survey*, London: MORI.
12 Mackenzie, C. (1993) *The Shareholder Action Book*, Newcastle: New Consumer.
13 Gallie, D. and White, M. (1993) *Employment in Britain Survey*, London: Department of Employment.
14 Wilson, A., Holton, V. and Handy, L. (1994) *The Ashridge Management Index 1994/95*, Berkhamstead: Ashridge Management Research Group.
15 Wilson, A. and Drummond, J. (1993) *The Importance of Being Ethical: Business Ethics and the Non-Executive Director*, Berkhamstead: Ashridge Management Research Group/Integrity Works.
16 Friedman, Milton (1962) *Capitalism and Freedom*, Chicago: University of Chicago Press, p. 133.
17 Zadek, S. and Evans, R. (1993) *Auditing the Market: A Practical Approach to Social Auditing*, Gateshead: Traidcraft Exchange.
18 Copies of their *Social Audit* are available from: Traidcraft Plc, Kingsway, Gateshead, Tyne and Wear, NE11 0NE.
19 Lloyd, Tom (1990) *The Nice Company*, London: Bloomsbury.

Part II

MICRO ISSUES

The relationship between the individual and the business organisation

INTRODUCTION TO PART II

Part II – *Micro Issues: The relationship between the individual and the business organisation*, has five contributions. As noted in the initial introduction, it is an increasingly important area due both to changing expectations, and to the fact that it is as an individual in an organisation that ethical dilemmas are often felt most acutely. In Chapter 5, *The Business Organisation: A locus for meaning and moral guidance*, Simon Webley starts from a simple question: should an employee follow his/her own ethics, or the company's, when trying to resolve an ethical dilemma? The issue is complicated by the decline in influence of both church and family which previously provided a greater commonality of expectations in terms of acceptable behaviour. He then examines various ways (e.g. codes and mission statements) in which companies try to promote a better match between individual values and those of the company. But, he argues, these are insufficient in a declining moral climate. The business organisation has already, for some, become a surrogate family, providing social and emotional support; should it now also take on the role of surrogate church with remedial moral training? Being a locus for moral guidance is not something businesses have actively sought (they have acquired it more by default), and there are genuine questions as to the legitimacy of their acting in these areas. But, given that such a high percentage of employees say they experience ethical problems in the workplace, it is not an issue that can be ignored. Companies will have to become more morally self-aware

61

and develop flexible family policies; such actions will speak louder than the usual feel-good rhetoric.

In Chapter 6, *The Psychological Contract: Enacting ethico-power*, Keith Pheby questions the hard binary (bureaucratic rationality) interpretation which sets 'the individual' and 'the organisation' against each other. He takes an autopoietic approach which sees organisations as self-referencing systems of communication with multiple rationalities, which enact their environment. He conjoins that other buzzword, 'empowerment', with ethics, to develop the notion of *ethico-power*. Organisations are distinct from individuals, but not powering over them; power is not a zero-sum game, but can be increased overall as the idea of ethico-power takes hold and enables organisations to cope ethically with creativity, diversity and difference – something they often say they want. However, this will require more democratic structures, more sharing of power and more trust in organisations. By viewing organisations explicitly as multiple realities, and by combining the notion of 'ethics' with 'empowerment', Keith Pheby opens the way to what a new psychological contract might look like for the late 1990s and beyond. It has some far-reaching implications, again bringing to the surface the issue of ownership.

In Chapter 7, *Acting Professionally: Something that business organisations and individuals both desire?*, Jane Pritchard questions the idea that greater professionalism is the way to get a greater match of values between individuals and organisations. Such an idea, she argues, is fallacious; the aims of business and professionalism are mutually exclusive – they have different motives. The motive for true professionals requires a focus on client need, and the delivery of tailor-made solutions for their clients' problems. The motive of business, however, is more financially oriented; trying to put the two together can only create conflicts of interest. Business should no more try to be professional, than the professions (she uses examples from the law and medicine) should try to be 'business-like'. For each to try to be like the other can only be harmful (though a diluted use of the word 'professional', as in 'doing a job well', has value). The way forward (ethically) for business is to change within its own value-system. It seems, then, that loose talk surrounding this notion of professionalism is really only adding to the confusion, but this is unlikely to deter the continuing efforts to appropriate this label as a means to gain public approval (look at how the 'profession' of accounting has benefited in terms of status and remuneration over the last twenty-five years, especially in contrast with, say, the engineering 'profession').

More concrete than an appeal to professional behaviour is the growing use of Company Codes of Ethics as a way of trying to help individuals and organisations live more comfortably with each other. In Chapter 8, *Codes of Ethics: Some uses and abuses*, Iain Munro looks at the role of codes. He argues that they have their uses in terms of PR and setting agendas, but cannot set priorities for many of the clashes of stakeholder interest – precisely the sorts of area where managers need positive guidance. This weakness is partly to do with how codes are formulated (often top-down, inspiring little commitment) and enforced (often inconsistently and from a punitive angle). Munro suggests that codes could be more fruitful if used as opportunities to understand the transgressor's viewpoint (one of the 'multiple realities', in Keith Pheby's language), and so contribute to building a moral dialogue. This is genuinely needed in order to address the hidden undercurrents (company culture) which are often the cause of dilemmas in the first place; codes can help lessen moral muteness in business organisations and, if fully exploited, provide an organisational mechanism to voice ethical concerns without fear of retaliation.

If no such organisational mechanism is provided, then its ultimate conclusion *may* be a case of whistleblowing, the final issue of Part II, explored by Angela Peek in Chapter 9, *Whistleblowing and its Alternatives*. Given no real mechanism to deal fully with ethical concerns, employees are left with a three-way choice: shut up (and swallow your conscience); get out (on the grounds of a severe mismatch of values); or blow the whistle (and take the very heavy consequences). It does appear that whistleblowers consider themselves to be loyal employees and, initially, never doubt that their concerns will be fully dealt with by senior management; they are often quite shocked to find the organisation 'turning against them'. The law currently fails to give adequate support (though the Public Interest Disclosure Bill being discussed at the time of writing should give greater protection if it becomes law). Codes are mentioned again, as being of limited help, and sources of external help are discussed. A whistleblower's checklist is finally outlined. But Peek argues that it is in everyone's interest to ensure that organisational procedures exist to minimise potential whistleblowing situations; using the notion of quality enhancement provides a common language in this respect.

The appeal of Part II is perhaps partly due to our individualist culture, where the individual (hero or villain) finds an identity either by fighting 'the system', or in some way coming to terms with the way things are within it. It covers the idea of the business organisation as a surrogate family and church, and the notion of ethico-power as a way of dealing with multiple realities; it has examined the desire for professionalism as a questionable organisational glue, and the concept of codes in a similar vein; and finally it has examined whistleblowing, which takes place when there is a failure in the above mechanisms. Many of the ideas in Part II seem to have been articulated in different guises in organisation theory, and so perhaps the emphasis should shift to implementation. The need for such action, though, will be made more acute by some of the longer-term, deeper trends that are happening both globally and within the UK. These are explored in Part III.

5

THE BUSINESS
ORGANISATION

A locus for meaning and moral guidance

Simon Webley

INTRODUCTION

On more than one occasion, in negotiating overseas contracts
in developing countries, I have had to decide whether or not to
meet the customer's request for a substantial 'commission' to
be paid to him personally. In each case the people involved
were senior government officials and the amounts were comparatively large. Payment invariably meant we would obtain
not only a profitable job but our employees in this country
needed the work. Do I accede to the requests?

This question, used in management training sessions to raise awareness of ethical issues, poses one of many dilemmas experienced by
managers in resolving day-to-day problems which have a moral
dimension. Indeed, problems involving choices of personal conduct
are faced by employees at all levels in the workplace on a daily basis.
Their resolution raises this question: 'Is the employee to adapt to
the organisation's ethos or to rely on their own values in resolving
moral problems they encounter at work?'

Two factors are crucial in determining how an organisation treats
issues of business conduct. First, the attitude of the leadership
(directors and senior management) to the individuals who are
employed in the business; and second, how employees view the role
and influence of the organisation in their lives. Because work occu-
pies a large percentage of their waking lives, do they expect it to
provide a significant level of *meaning and satisfaction*, or is it seen
merely as a means to produce an income?

One common way of describing the role of business organisations of any size is as a set of relationships with other organisations

(banks, suppliers, other businesses, etc.) and with individuals – principally customers and employees.

LAW OF CONTRACT

These relationships have a foundation in law – the law of contract being the most familiar.[1] The formal legal relationship provides a protection for both employees and employers. In the case of employees based in the United Kingdom, a contract of employment setting out the terms and conditions of employment is required by law to be given to all staff. Such contracts vary in content, but they provide guidance for both employer and employee on their rights and obligations to each other. The contract tends to be standardised and conventional, and is perhaps more a statement of status than a contract.[2]

Research has shown that employers have an ambivalent attitude to the introduction of anything more than the most formal statements in any contract with employees. A survey of one hundred UK-based companies known to have codes of business ethics showed that only 46 per cent included a reference to them in their employees' contracts of employment.[3]

But a strictly legal relationship between a business and its stakeholders, particularly its employees, is invoked only in the unusual situation of a dispute. It lays down certain minimum procedures (length of notice, amount of compensation, etc.); it does not set out to address more than the basic relationship, and it rarely has any reference to the values of the business let alone the values of an employee.

BUSINESS VALUES

Business values cannot easily be reduced to writing. In recent years, the increase in the numbers of organisations producing statements of purpose (mission statements) has enabled observers to discern what boards of directors expect from the employees of corporations. Most statements amount to a set of aspirations – a useful means of showing those who want to know that the organisation has purpose and direction. Only when such statements go on to form the basis of clear codes of good practice or ethics do they really have any effect on the behaviour of employees and corporations, and then often in a negative way (for example, in the resolution of disciplinary matters).

THE VALUE OF STAFF

Mission statements are not the only way that employers seek to set out business values and direction. In most companies' annual reports there is a paragraph in the Chairman's Statement saying how valuable the staff is to the organisation. An example illustrates the point:

> People are crucial to our business and we continue to invest in extensive training programmes and to establish clear objectives to enable them to achieve the Group's goals as well as their own. My thanks go to all our employees for their significant contribution.
> (J. M. K Laing, Chairman, John Laing Plc, Annual Report, 1995)

Board members hope that statements like this will have the effect of assuring employees that they are valued, especially when this is reflected in the pay packet and in positive annual appraisals. It is not a substitute for giving purpose to work, and it does not address the need for moral guidance when solving problems encountered in the course of day-to-day business.

It is in the production and implementation of codes of business ethics that some of these dilemmas are being addressed in a useful and positive way (see Chapter 8). Introductions to such codes, usually signed by the Chairman or CEO, tend to be much more explicit about business values than other public documents emanating from companies. An illustration of this is in the Introduction to United Biscuits' document, 'Ethics and Operating Principles':

> United Biscuits' business ethics are not negotiable – a well-founded reputation for scrupulous dealing is itself a priceless company asset and the most important single factor in our success is faithful adherence to our beliefs. While our tactical plans and many other elements constantly change, our basic philosophy does not. To meet the challenges of a changing world, we are prepared to change everything about ourselves except our values.

Some employees might have the mistaken idea that we do not care how results are obtained, as long as we get results. This would be wrong: we do care how we get results. We expect compliance with our standard of integrity throughout the company, and we will support an employee who passes up an opportunity or advantage which can only be secured at the sacrifice of principle.[4]

Where businesses have similar publicly stated values, there is a basis for expecting relationships at all levels to reflect these ideals. Most codes have sections dealing specifically with the company's relationship with its employees. These address specific areas of behaviour and give guidance to resolving moral dilemmas at work.

MAINTAINING THE RIGHTS OF EMPLOYEES

The surge in recent years in formal (contract) and informal (code of practice) statements of relationships between employer and employee has reflected a growing need for translating macro-level aspirations to the micro level – the place of work. The larger the organisation, the greater the need becomes to recognise that the system, which often plays a dominant role in the lives of employees, is in danger of treating them as mere factors of production. Individual opinions, or even rights, tend to be subjugated to that of the organisation for which one works. When employment opportunities are scarce, few speak up to voice concern for what is happening should they wish to do so.

To counter this, trade unions have provided a focus of protest – or at least a means by which employees can express their views corporately. Much of the industrial unrest in the United Kingdom in the 1960s and 1970s was an expression of frustration with the anonymity of working on repetitive processes in impersonal, and often depressing, places of work.

Two reactions followed. First, many large monopolistic organisations were broken down into smaller units and, when in the public sector, denationalised. Second, the application of new management techniques originating in Sweden and Japan, together with new technological processes, meant that work was tending to be organised in smaller groups with shared skills and delegated responsibility. Changes in the law on the conduct of industrial disputes and higher standards of health and safety at work have contributed to the transformation of relations between individuals and management for the better.[5]

ETHICAL STANDARD

Beside these changes affecting the employee at his or her place of work, observers have noticed an important social trend in the relationship of the corporation to society. The company is increasingly assuming a role as an upholder of ethical norms in the community.

It is apparent that general moral standards in Western countries are deteriorating. This phenomenon has been well documented and affects businesses in a number of ways. For instance, pilfering from retail stores in the United Kingdom has reached epidemic proportions. The British Retail Consortium estimates that two and a half billion pounds are lost per annum from stealing in retail stores. In response, increasing amounts are being invested in security systems which eventually have to be reflected in the price of products. Marks & Spencer, the UK retail chain, reports that it loses £30 million a year because of crime, and spends an additional £21 million a year combating crime of all sorts, which amounts to an extra penny in the pound (1 per cent) on the prices of its products.[6]

The decline in the moral climate is also reflected in the standard of integrity of employees of all levels within the place of work. The rise in the level of complaints by supervisors and other managers about the basic honesty, discipline and respect for others of many junior employees has led to the introduction of the topic of ethical behaviour into induction courses for new staff. Paradoxically, it is the failure to impart moral values by traditional agents in society – family, school, church or other religious institutions – which is forcing the business sector to provide help in achieving minimum acceptable standards of behaviour at the workplace. Professor Jack Mahoney has pointed out that Adam Smith and Montesquieu, among others, saw business as a humanising influence in society.[7] Mahoney himself sees no reason why this should not be encouraged. Yet, for centuries, Blake's 'dark satanic mills' and Dickens's depiction of a Victorian office in *A Christmas Carol* have been prevailing images, with all their attendant implications for appalling conditions at the place of work (which were very often justified). The resurgence of this role for the company, largely to fill a moral vacuum, puts special demands on senior executives. It is not surprising that some are asking 'who is to act as the moral guide for the company?' This question becomes even more important in the case of multinational companies (see Chapter 10).

Social scientists point out that 'going to work' plays a significant function in the social and moral wellbeing of employees. Studies of those who are unable to find work after being 'laid off' reveal a pattern of social withdrawal after, say, six months; similar observations have been made of those who experience abrupt retirement. The place of work has, to many, become something of a surrogate family. This dependency has implications for company policy, especially in the handling of change. In an age of rapid response to changing market conditions, loyalty to an employing company has become a largely devalued concept.

Driven by both legislation and ethical consideration, responsible employers now provide working conditions far removed from those dark satanic mills. At the same time, they find themselves forced to address ethical issues concerning their staff. The workplace is increasingly seen as a place where human and social values are being cultivated – it is realised by many business leaders to be both good business sense, and good citizenship, to take account of this phenomenon. But not every business relishes this role, and some tend to be resentful of a system that forces them to do moral remedial work on the young people joining their workforce. Failure of the traditional conduits of ethical values is seen by them as a major issue which needs addressing at the highest level; they argue that most businesses feel ill-equipped to address the problem.

WHAT ARE THE VALUES OF BUSINESS?

If it is true that businesses are being forced to play an increasing role in setting or maintaining moral standards in society, then it is important to be clear about what values are inherent in them. An examination of company statements about their values shows certain recurring themes and a few 'value laden' words. These include 'honest', 'truth', 'reputation', 'responsible' and 'integrity'. Few business leaders would disassociate themselves or their organisations from these concepts, though there seems to be a general reluctance to be too explicit, especially outside the United States where ethics and values play a major part in the style of business culture. Whereas US companies seem to make a point of preparing their organisation for occasions when issues of corporate moral behaviour arise, the majority of UK corporations seem content to make broad statements about business integrity. Comparatively few have translated their corporate values into corporate codes. The 1991 survey of the Institute of Business Ethics estimates that less than one in three of the larger United Kingdom companies have a code of business ethics, though the number is growing.[8]

Attempts have been made to discern the values which characterise corporations and their leaders. One method used was to record broad reactions to normal business challenges. Reidenbach and Robin have classified corporate attitudes in the United States in five stages, as follows:

- *Amoral* – devoid of any other value than greed
- *Legalistic* – whatever is legal is OK
- *Responsive* – enlightened self interest guides decisions
- *Emerging Ethical* – we wish to do what is right
- *Ethical* – core values characterise all policies[9]

A similar classification based on surveys from the 1970s put them like this:

- *Laissez faire* – 'All is fair in love, war and business'
- *Relativist* – 'Good ethics is good business'
- *Legalistic* – 'We operate according to clear rules'
- *Virtuous* – 'We have obligations for which we are accountable'[10]

There is a growing interest from moral philosophers in this area. They bring with them models of human behaviour[11] which have been used to classify different attitudes and values. There seems to be no clear agreement as to which theory best fits observed business behaviour. As a result, business ethics is seen as not that relevant to real-life situations. Andrew Start, in his seminal article on business ethics in the Harvard Business Review of May 1993, observed that 'most people's motives are a confusing mix of self interest, altruism and other influences'.[12]

PRACTICAL GUIDANCE

What managers say they require is some practical means to resolve conflicts between economic reality and employees' wish to act as moral human beings. They argue that they are not free to be altruistic because they manage companies *on behalf of* others. On the other hand, they know that, in the long term, doing the right thing is good for the corporation. The following threefold test has been offered to help resolve the ethics of a decision:

- *Effect* – Who does my decision effect or hurt?
- *Transparency* – Do I mind others knowing what I have decided?
- *Fairness* – Would my decision be considered fair by those affected?[13]

Some business organisations are now producing tests of this sort. For instance, the National Westminster Bank says:

Key questions which may help understanding of the ethical aspects of our dealings with customers and suppliers include:

- do our actions or proposed actions fall comfortably within Group guidelines, the consensus view of what constitutes ethical behaviour and generally accepted concepts of fairness and honesty?
- might our actions mislead or raise expectations which cannot be fulfilled?
- would our customer or supplier have any cause for grievance if the full extent of our actions were apparent to them?
- would we have any sense of grievance if we had been treated similarly?
- would an impartial observer regard our dealings as fair and honourable?[14]

British Petroleum states that:

Within BP the general principles of individual ethical behaviour include:

- the scrupulous avoidance of deception, 'sharp practice' fraud and of any behaviour which is or might be construed to be less than honourable in the pursuit of the Group's commercial interest.
- honesty in dealings with BP as employer, and loyalty to BP above any and all temptations to pursue personal gain or advantage.
- honesty and loyalty in dealing with fellow employees.
- respect for the trust placed in the individual including proper use of Group resources of information.

- avoidance of the behaviour or situations which may reflect badly on BP.[15]

The value words which recur in the two companies' statements are 'fairness', 'honesty', 'respect', 'honourable', 'loyalty' and 'trust', while the word 'reputation' is implied. These words are frequently encountered in business statements and are important in establishing the prevailing ethos of the organisation. This becomes particularly important for corporations which are transnational. Whereas a code may be useful and enforceable in a national context, the value system implied in it may be inappropriate and different elsewhere. Little is known about this.

ISSUES IN THE FUTURE

It was pointed out earlier that the corporation for some, acts as a surrogate family. Paradoxically it is family policy issues that are likely to become more important for companies in the coming years. The retention of technically and managerially able staff by the organisation will become an important part of the strategy of any successful company. Obviously, remuneration packages will reflect this, but so also will any company's attitude to family life. Furthermore, there is a growing concern at national level about the effect on the family of the demands of the workplace on employees. This interest is being driven by sociologists, who are concerned about the increasing breakdown of the family and its effect on children, and by the medical profession, which is concerned about the increase in mental illness, including stress-related illness, in those of working age. Concern is being expressed about the amount of time employees are required to be absent from their families. This may cause stress either because employees have to work at a location a long distance from their home, or because of compulsory overtime or work practices which require voluntary overtime, both of which disrupt family life. In a recent survey of UK company practice on employee health, Firth-Cozens has shown that companies are generally slow to develop policies on the family.[16] By such policies she means: provision of on-site or other assistance with child care facilities; flexible working; career breaks; parental leave schemes; job sharing; and family days and spouse involvement generally. It would be sensible if businesses took the lead on this matter rather than having to react to the agendas of others.

SUMMARY

Employees at all levels experience moral issues in the workplace. These may be different in nature depending on their level in the business organisation, but some guidance on how to respond in such situations is needed if the integrity of the organisation and the employee is to be maintained. The contract of employment is a starting point but, as such, it does not reflect the values of corporations or give meaning to work. Business values are best judged by the actions taken by corporations, as well as by their written or oral statements. The issues are practical, changing only according to size or sector of business operation. For instance, payment of invoices on time by large corporations is often critical for the survival of smaller firms; and smaller firms can have a detrimental effect on tax payers by the prevalence of unrecorded cash transactions.

It is generally agreed that ethical standards in society are slipping, and this is reflected in behaviour at the work place. Companies are increasingly seeing the necessity of filling the moral vacuum by some sort of 'remedial training' (e.g. the setting of company values, and/or the circulation of ethical guidelines). This appears to be because family, school and church are no longer effectively fulfilling this role.

It is important to know what business leaders' values are and what moral guidance is being offered to employees, especially when there is constant and increasing pressure for survival (wrapped up in the more legitimate-sounding language of strategy – 'gaining competitive advantage', etc.). In other words, companies will have to become more morally self-aware. Work can be a way of giving a meaning to life but it can also be a place of anxiety and stress. If the maintenance of healthy family life is to be a national policy objective, some business practices which disrupt families will increasingly be questioned. Large companies often have family policies, but the small and medium-sized companies protest that they cannot afford them. Perhaps such a situation is endemic to a market-oriented system, but the warning signs are there and it is in everyone's interest to face these issues.

NOTES

1 For a discussion of these issues, see Fincham R. and Rhodes P. S. (1992) *The Individual, Work and Organisation* (2nd edn), London: Weidenfeld & Nicolson.

2 For a detailed discussion of the legal relations between employers and employees, see Davies, Paul and Freedand, Mark (1984) *Labour Law, Text and Materials* (2nd edn), London: Weidenfeld & Nicolson, chapter 3; see also Whincup, Michael (1991) *Modern Employment Law* (7th edn), Oxford: Butterworth–Heinemann, chapter 2.

3 Webley, Simon (1995) *Use of Codes of Conduct in UK Based Organisations*, London: Institute of Business Ethics.

4 See United Biscuits (1987) *Ethics and Operating Principles*.

5 For detailed descriptions of this process, see Handy, Charles (1984) *The Future of Work*, Oxford: Blackwell; see also Barley, Stephen R. (1995) *The New World of Work*, London: British–North American Committee.

6 For more such details, see the *National Survey of Retail Theft and Security*, produced by the Nene College School of Business, 1994.

7 Mahoney, Jack (1993) 'Business to the Rescue', *Business Ethics: A European Review*, 2(3), pp. 109–10.

8 Webley, Simon (1992) *Business Ethics and Company Codes*, London: Institute of Business Ethics.

9 Reidenbach, Eric and Robin, Donald (1991) 'Conceptual Model of Corporate Moral Development', *Journal of Business Ethics*, 10(4), pp. 273–84.

10 For instance, see Baumhart, Raymond (1968) *An Honest Profit*, New York: Holt, Reinhard and Winston; see also Webley, Simon (1971) *British Businessmen's Behaviour*, London: Foundation for Business Responsibilities.

11 For a summary of this topic, see Warren, Richard (1993) 'Codes of Ethics: Bricks Without Straw', *Business Ethics*, 2(4), pp. 185–91.

12 Start, Andrew (1993) 'What's the Matter with Business Ethics', *Harvard Business Review*, May/June, 71(3), pp. 38–41, 44, 46, 48 (quote is from p. 41).

13 Webley, Simon (1994) 'Business Ethics are on the Agenda', *Business News*, (City University Business School), May, pp. 3–5.

14 National Westminster Bank (1993) *It's Good Business*.

15 British Petroleum (1990) *Policy on Business Conduct*.

16 Firth-Cozens, Jenny (1995) *Employees' Health and Organisational Practice*, London: Institute of Business Ethics.

6

THE PSYCHOLOGICAL CONTRACT

Enacting ethico-power

Keith Pheby

INTRODUCTION

During the last two decades, two notions have increasingly come into vogue with respect to organisational life: ethics and empowerment. While it has been tacitly assumed that there exists a close connection between them, as yet no attempt has been made explicitly to map the contours of their interrelation. This contribution is an attempt partially to fill this lacuna by articulating a conceptual space for the realisation of what will be referred to as *ethico-power*. It will be argued that a new psychological contract must be developed which allows for the realisation of individual creativity, diversity and difference.

Of course, these themes are not new. Advocates of *industrial democracy,*[1] of *empowerment,*[2] not to mention a veritable host of Organisational Development theorists and practitioners, have addressed many of the issues to be revisited in this chapter. However, one of the main criticisms of the deployment of these inherently ethical ideas in the organisational domain has been their lack of a coherent theoretical framework, necessary to overcome the charges of naïvety and wishful thinking. Alternative perspectives on organisation arrangements, arrangements, that is, that attempt to break with the predominance of bureaucratic rationality in favour of multiple rationalities, have been continually attacked as bearing no relation to organisational reality. A deficit of empirical evidence, and controversial theoretical constructions which appear too abstract and general, are the main bones of contention. This chapter will not pretend to provide empirical evidence for its claims but hopefully will provide a conceptual framework within which the relationship between ethics and power can be coherently articulated.

76

AUTOPOIESIS AND CONTEXTUALISED AUTONOMY

One of the benefits of the *autopoietic* approach is that it allows us to construe organisations as intentional entities or, to be more precise, intentional fields, without denying the autonomy of the individual organisational member. As Morgan has noted, 'traditional approaches to organisation theory have been dominated by the idea that change originates in the environment . . . the organisation is typically viewed as an open system in constant interaction with its context . . . changes in the environment are viewed as presenting challenges to which the organisation must respond'.[3] Thus, the organisation enters into a relation of linear causality with its environment which imposes a range of demands to which the organisation must respond if it is to survive. Contingency theory, population ecology and the labour process theorists conceive of the organisation as the dependent term of this relation. By contrast, from the autopoietic perspective, organisations are self-referencing systems of communication which do not merely receive information from the environment but are also proactive in changing that environment as well. As Wheatley puts it, 'No part of the larger system is left unaffected by changes that occur someplace within it – co-evolution'.[4]

Organisations need to attain a certain level of self-referentiality if they are to be able to enact their own environment; to project the internal value system outward. The environment should not be construed as an amorphous mass, a singular entity, standing over and above the specific system under consideration. Systems form *structural couplings*,[5] and networks of these couplings are precisely what constitutes the notion of environment. They are governed by a process of mutual causality, and any attempt to demarcate a site of differentiation, between system and environment, will always be the result of an arbitrary choice to break the circular pattern of interaction. Of course, for organisations, the choice can be a 'conscious' one. They can be seen as 'points of view' enacting their environments in terms of their internal modes of operation; creating identities through processes of reality construction.

Autopoeisis radically complicates both the relation between organisations and the relations holding between the organisation and its membership, each conceived in terms of what we will refer to as *contextualised autonomy*. Organisations maintain identities that are quantitatively distinct from the aggregate of individual desires and preferences. That is, they are not reducible to the interests of individual organisational members conceived as autonomous agents. However, this is not to suggest that organisations stand over and above individuals or groups of individuals as an 'objective' structure. The individual organisational member is never merely subservient and reactive *vis-à-vis* the organisation, any more than the organisation is subservient to the demands of an estranged and overbearing environment. Individuals form circular patterns of interaction which, at a certain level, consolidate to form a discrete organisational whole. The contextualised nature of individual autonomy provided by autopoiesis sidesteps the accusation, levelled by what we might call for the want of a better phrase the 'humanist' camp, that the individual in systems theoretic discussions is redundant. The self is not being replaced in favour of structure, but displaced and resituated.

The integrity of organisations, that is their ability to maintain a certain difference, a certain identity, depends upon their ability to consolidate that difference in terms of articulating a domain of shared meaning. At the heart of this structural closure lie processes of communication, operating internally by defining a common conceptual framework for the realisation of common desires, and operating externally by a process of reality construction which determines the organisation's mode of interaction with other systems within its domain. Indeed, through autopoeisis, inter-organisational relations appear as an intricate web of which the 'elements' are continually and continuously affecting and being affected by other elements. Understanding the nature of these processes of communication will greatly aid the current debates concerning inter-organisational collaboration and cooperation.

Autopoeisis provides the theoretical framework for re-thinking the system–environment relation. But, even construed in terms of circular patterns of interaction, the complexity contained in such a network of relations threatens to overwhelm any particular system, either at the individual or organisational level, unless mechanisms for its reduction can be successfully utilised. All systems require mechanisms capable of reducing complexity in order both to maintain stability and to optimise the field of possible action. Social complexity is dealt with in terms of maintaining the *identity*, *definition* and *stability* of these action systems. A strong corporate culture, aware of its bedrock of shared meaning, is in a better position to cope with *intersystemic noise* than is a corporate milieu premised on functional bifurcation and riddled with a fragmentation of goals.

It hardly needs stating that, in traditional bureaucratic structures, the two inevitably go hand-in-hand. The veneer of conformity they display through processes of socialisation based on adherence to the instrumentally rational principles of calculability, predictability and control, is undercut and exploded at the very time when it is most needed – during times of crisis and chaos. Bureaucracies seldom exhibit the robust bonding mechanisms based upon substantive matrices of shared meaning that would be necessary to sustain them in uncertain environments. These are environments in which the circular patterns of interaction exhibit a high speed of combination and recombination. Part of the reason for this is the generally acknowledged propensity of bureaucratic structures to succumb to segmentalism,[6] with each department, function or, indeed, in the case of the more seriously afflicted organisations, each individual following disparate and often incommensurable agendas. The result is a decoupling process within the systemic network where the inherent fragility of the organisation, *qua* systemic matrix, becomes increasingly entropic. This tendency is partly due to the view that the human subject is an isolated, atomised entity. However, conceptions of subjectivity are generated by dominant structures, or modes of structuration, which form and are sustained within particular cultures. The form of homogenised individualism imposed upon the members of bureaucracies does violence to the potential creative self-expression of human subjectivity. It is important to recognise that the human subject is a dynamic, thoroughly historical construct. Bureaucracies attempt artificially to freeze that dynamism by transforming individuals into sites for the expression of an organised rationality dedicated to the realisation of sectional interests and values. It is necessary to adumbrate a notion of social bonding which avoids recourse to this instrumentalisation of the individual as the point of departure.

Before turning to discuss the ways in which this *contextualised autonomy* is implicated in the notion of ethico-power, we need to state precisely the way in which the notion of *power* is being deployed. The autopoietic approach depersonalises power and opens the power system for use by all organisational participants without collapsing into a zero-sum game. Insisting that power in social systems be construed in terms of 'power over', results in a situation where an increase in the power of one person must necessarily be obtained at the expense of another. To the extent that one person gains power, there is a tendency to think that another or others must lose it. However, 'power over' does not conceptually exhaust the domain of power. The grammatical complexity of the term 'power'[7] opens up the possibility of weaving a cluster of characteristics appropriate to the purpose of constructing organisational power systems capable of releasing ethico-power. It will be argued, following Wittgenstein, that power is a family resemblance concept[8] and, as such, any search for the *essence* of power is doomed to failure from the start. Our concern, therefore, will be exclusively with productive power, and this will necessarily entail bracketing any analysis of the varying merits of competing theories of the nature of what we can term oppressive power. However, the general point can be made that the classical view of power construes the phenomenon in terms of oppressive imbalances in interpersonal relations and relies upon a particular intellectual construct and a particular pattern of ritualised behaviour known as the *market*. This can be defined as 'a spontaneous and self-adjusting order which emerges from the exchanges of benefits between self-interested individuals'.[9] The insistence on its naturalness seems to militate against the possibility of construing power in a way that does not include the factor of coercion as externally related individuals compete to realise their own self-interests. That is, what is lost is the possibility of productive power.

Releasing ethico-power requires an understanding of complex patterns of connectivity[10] and an appreciation of the way in which organisations maintain their identity. It is now time to turn to the discussion of ethico-power, re-evoking the notions of contextualised autonomy and autopoiesis addressed earlier.

ETHICO-POWER

There is a growing body of evidence which suggests that there is a demand, not only for higher standards of business conduct, but for an unprecedented leap in terms of ethics and quality of values, both within and between organisations as well as between organisations and their respective communities.[11] It will be argued in what follows that this leap should be construed as a qualitative one and not merely as a demand for a greater proliferation of traditional ethical values within the socius. A new, or at least a revitalised, cluster of ethical concepts is required that is appropriate to current organisational life. These concepts are embedded implicitly within the democratic ideals of society at large and can, given the right structural conditions, be made explicit within organisations. Organisations should not be seen merely as reflecting and responding to the ethical values prevalent in and determined by the current philosophical literature or the current socio-political milieu. Rather, they should be proactive in developing and expanding them.[12] Organisational life has the potential to promote a moral sensitivity which can then be utilised to stimulate a more general enthusiasm for a positive intervention into the democratic processes of society at large. There is no *a priori* reason why organisations should not be sites of development for the realisation of a thoroughly participative form of democracy. The potential of direct forms of participation in corporations has ramifications that extend far beyond the mere increase in productivity. Mutual causality characterises intersystemic relations at all levels, and this suggests that ethical interventions at one level will have a ripple effect, affecting the entire inter- and intra-organisational domain.

Thus, an ethics of organisations, if it is to ground the desire to realise the empowering of individuals in a truly social context, must inform as well as reflect the values that are implicit in the idea of democracy. The ethical vocabulary deployed here will not be based either on the autonomous subject, nor on time-independent normative values. It is hoped that the notion of contextualised autonomy has addressed the first part of the humanist's disquiet. The majority of ethical systems are premised on the assumption of individual responsibility. Inherent in this view is the assumption that obligations and rights accrue primarily to autonomous agents. Already in place is the belief, which is being critiqued here, that subjects are externally rather than internally related (in the sense of inhabiting a shared context, a common life-world). Furthermore, morality is defined by its alienated character: it is typically expressed as a set of external requirements to which the individual must conform. It is these notions of externality and alienation *vis-à-vis* moral responsibility which must be overcome.

With regard to the lack of time invariance, the ethical cluster being developed in this chapter makes no reference to transcendence. Ethico-power is being constructed from a coherent, yet not necessarily predominant, pool of shared values, extant within society at large. However, this position is not merely based on an exhortation to shared values. It will be argued that ethico-power conforms to general practical/prudential needs of organisational life. Thus, ethico-power avoids taking recourse to an ethical tradition which privileges any variety of moral absolutism which, as far as the organisational context is concerned, is either unworkable or irrelevant to those organisational members to which it is supposed to apply. Given that societies are dynamic systems, the domain of values to which they give rise cannot, by definition, be transcendent. However, the fact that this domain is subject to the vagaries of time in no way diminishes its capacity to produce a set of ethical postulates.

Certain notions are indispensable (if not presently realisable) to ensure that organisations truly reflect the democratic ideals supposedly upheld in the community. First, *reciprocity*, explicated in terms of the sphere of reciprocal interactions referred to above as contextualised autonomy. Second, *responsibility*, a notion which needs to be retrieved, both from the Utilitarian framework where it functions as a corrective to the narrowly instrumental interests of atomised subjects, and from the deontological predisposition to construe the notion in terms of the obligations/rights/duties axis. The term 'responsibility' signifies, like any other term, within a context; and, perhaps more forcefully, no particular context ever saturates the term's possibility of signification. The motivation for the responsibility required by ethico-power is not dependent upon imperatives or the imposition of moral commands. It is not generated by a code or system but is a mode of 'responding' which flows directly out of the respect for difference which lies at the heart of democracy.

It has been shown that it is difficult to divorce the desire to develop ethical organisational cultures from an analysis of the structures which are essential for their realisation. Bureaucracy, utilitarianism and instrumental rationality form a conceptual cluster which seriously impedes the transformation of organisations from technical utility maximising machines into structures capable of generating and sustaining ethico-power. There needs to be a gap in the control process large enough to allow organisational members the space to enact processes and pursue trajectories outside of the domain dictated by technical reason. Reed has suggested that the 'ontological status of "organisation" as enacted process, rather than imposed structure, has emerged as a central strand of thinking in contemporary organisational analysis'.[13] This is supported by Giddens's recent arguments in which 'the theory of structuration is invoked and deployed in the attempt to develop explanatory logics encompassing both the enabling or empowering aspects of "structure", as well as its constraining or limiting influence'.[14] This approach is supported by the autopoietic arguments presented earlier in this chapter.

Ethico-power demands an open and participative organisational culture which recognises the mutual causality which determines relations at every level. This requires an equally open and participative structure. Sustaining an ethical culture, whether it be within or between organisations, also means that those patterns express a commitment to a general cluster of ethical values. Despite the fact that there appears to be a general and somewhat unfounded cynicism in some quarters concerning the genuine possibility of an ethical transformation of corporate life, one factor might persuade even the most recalcitrant. Faced with chaotic environments, many organisations will have no option other than to deploy strategies which successfully reduce complexity. Sharing power is a necessary element in this project. Such sharing depends on the existence of the corollary notions of collaboration, cooperation and partnership which, in their turn, depend upon *trust*. Trust is necessary to sustain cooperative relationships. Dependent parties need some degree of assurance that non-dependent parties will not defect. Furthermore, in general, people will not trust others enough to bring about cooperation unless their assurance is to some extent well based; that is to say, unless people are also in general motivated, one way or another, not to defect if they are in a non-dependent position. This will only be possible if a higher level of individual and collective consciousness can be generated which calls for a sharing of meaning. Open communication is of the essence.

The greater the complexity the greater the call for new mechanisms for its reduction. Trust is one such mechanism. One cannot manage chaos; no system can totally match the complexity of its environment, conceived as a mosaic of self-regulating systems. However, trust can act as a medium for partial reduction inasmuch as it acts to exclude a certain range of unpredictable actions on the part of others. The lack of trust decreases the possibility for variety of action and thus stifles the creative promulgation of innovative and potentially mutually empowering decision-making in the action domain.

Whatever decisions are made, and whatever actions are the result of that decision-making process, will entail *patterns of motivation* and *structures of expectations* that are informed by their relevance to others, inasmuch as they are affected by them, and by the recognition that such acting will not be rendered impotent by their negative intervention. The greater the complexity of the system the greater the multiplicity of ways of generating trust which is inextricably linked to the successful building of predictable patterns of communication. It is of even more importance in novel circumstances such as those that appear in the chaotic environment of organisations. Such an environment typifies the organisation attempting to throw off the trappings of bureaucratic hierarchies, faced as it is with the task of managing the expectations of its members, many of whom will see such change as a threat. These considerations can be reinforced by the fact that there is also an individual psychological need for a reduction in ambiguity in our relations with others.

Ethico-power can only flourish in an organisational milieu characterised by trust, open systems of communication and the non-existence of forms of oppressive power. Participative democracy demands that all the diverse groups which constitute an organisation have a right to take part in the policy-making decisions that affect them. All values must be taken into account. Generating a distinct organisational identity, fulfilling the autopoietic requirements for systems growth, can only proceed if patterns of shared meaning are developed, and this means taking into account the value and belief systems of all participants, respecting difference and diversity. Mechanisms of trust can only be sustained if organisational members do not feel excluded. Individual desires, preferences and interests must be taken into consideration. It cannot be assumed that they will constitute a homogenous set. However, criteria must be established which are to govern our interpersonal relations within the organisational context.

Given the innate temporality of the human subject, individuals have to create and re-create themselves. Similarly, organisations, construed as individuals at a different level of systemic closure, are continually developing, changing and enacting their environments. If collective life is not to become sterile and suffocating, organisations must embrace an openness to the new – and must have the opportunity to create new forms of interaction. Organisations must never be perceived as being sites of normalisation/manipulation by their members, and this can only be avoided by allowing power to circulate in as free a way as possible. The enactment of ethico-power is required by the systemic imperative of autopoiesis as well as by the ethical demand that difference and diversity are respected.

NOTES

1 See Poole, Michael (1986) *Towards a New Industrial Democracy: Workers' Participation in Industry*, London: Routledge & Kegan Paul; Brannen, P. (1983) *Authority and Participation in Industry*, London: Batsford; Elliott, J. (1984) *Conflict or Cooperation? The Growth of Industrial Democracy* (revised edn), London: Kogan Page.

2 In particular the work of Rosabeth Moss Kanter: for example Kanter, R. M. (1983) *The Changemasters*, New York: Simon and Schuster.

3 Morgan, Gareth (1986) *Images of Organisation*, Beverly Hills, Cal: Sage, pp. 235–6.

4 Wheatley, Margaret J. (1994) *Leadership and the New Science*, San Francisco: Berrett-Koehler, p. 97.

5 Luhman, Niklas (1992) 'Operational Closure and Structural Coupling: The Differentiation of the Legal System', *Cardozo Law Review*, 13, p. 1419.

6 Kanter, *The Changemasters*.

7 Even a cursory examination of the literature concerning the nature of power reveals that any universality in defining the concept will inevitably be challenged. Power is seen as an ability to affect, an ability to mobilise, a capacity to exert influence, an ability to employ sanction and so on. For an overview on the concept, see Barnes, Barry (1988) *The Nature of Power*, Cambridge, Polity Press.

8 In the *Philosophical Investigations* (1953), Wittgenstein warns against the view that everything designated by a particular word must necessarily have something in common: an essence. Using the example of games he suggests that, rather than assuming that games must have something in common or they couldn't be called 'games', we should *look* and *see* whether there is anything common. 'For if you look at them you will not see something that is common to *all*, but similarities, relationships, and a whole series of them at that. To repeat: don't think, but look.'

9 Lively, Jack (1976) 'The Limits of Exchange Theory', in Barry, Brian (ed.), *Power and Political Theory*, London: Wiley, p. 1.

10 These patterns are currently being explored in a longer work on ethico-power.

11 However, despite this growing trend towards taking ethics seriously, European corporations are still significantly behind the USA in introducing codes of ethics and similar corporate statements. While it has been argued that European corporations seem to be introducing codes at a rate that will bring them to a level reported by US companies in the mid-1980s by 1996, the subjects addressed by corporate codes differ strikingly between Europe and the US. The Catherine C. Langlois and Bodo B. Schlegelmich survey 'Journal of International Business' found that, whereas 100 per cent of the European codes surveyed addressed the subject of employee conduct, the same was true for only 55 per cent of the US codes. Ninety-six per cent of the US codes dealt with political/government relations. The same was true for only 15 per cent of the European codes. Eighty-six per cent of US codes

addressed relationships with suppliers and contractors, as against only 19 per cent of the European codes. The topic of customer relations was addressed by 81 per cent of the US codes. This was where the major difference was found between the European countries: whereas only 39 per cent of the UK codes mentioned this topic, customers were included in 67 per cent of the German codes and 93 per cent of the French codes. Community and environment was another topic where a difference was found: 65 per cent of European codes mentioned it against 42 per cent of the US codes. With respect to innovation and technology, 60 per cent of the European codes included this against 42 per cent of the US codes. With respect to innovation and technology 60 per cent of the German codes included this; 20 per cent in the French codes, 15 per cent in the US and 6 per cent in British companies.

12 The 1992 announcement of the Cooperative Bank's Ethical Policy is an example of a corporation not only responding to the demands of its customers but actively seeking to enhance an ethical sensitivity within the community.

13 Reed, Michael I (1992) *The Sociology of Organisations: Themes, Perspective and Prospects*, Hemel Hempstead, Herts: Harvester Wheatsheaf, p. 185.

14 Ibid., p. 187.

7

ACTING PROFESSIONALLY

Something that business organisations and individuals both desire?

Jane Pritchard

INTRODUCTION

In the sense that 'acting professionally' means doing the job well, no-one would deny that the question in the title of this chapter should be answered in the affirmative. However, it is not so straight-forward to say that it is desirable for business to be 'professional' in the sense that 'acting professionally' means to act like a doctor or a lawyer. This chapter will show that the values of business are different from those of the professions, and that the respective aims of business and professionalism are to a large extent mutually exclusive. Why is business trying to promote itself as a profession? It may be that recent assertions that business is a profession[1] are a means of establishing a higher status for business in our society. This means not only enhanced social standing but also the enhanced moral standing traditionally given to professionals, who have had to be 'fit and proper persons' in order to be allowed to become members of their professional bodies.

This chapter will argue that trying to be professional is the wrong route: business should achieve merit in its own right and can be ethical without being professional. But, as will be argued, being moral is 'detachable' from business, whereas it is intrinsic to professionalism. Increasingly, too, the professions are anxious to show that they are 'business-like'. It will be argued that for professionals to do this defeats the true aims of a profession. If the name of business is to be associated in the future with ethical practices, business must behave morally within its own terms and according to its own values.

What, then, is a profession? This chapter will maintain that a profession must have an unshakeable aspiration to use its knowledge for the good of a client, and that this aspiration is liable to clash with a profit motive. The proper motive of business is profit, and thus there will be a conflict of interest if business is constructed like a profession. In addition, a profession must not jeopardise its essential aims by pretending to be a business. Some professional roles are very lucrative – for example, that of the tax lawyer – but others are not: the average clergyman is barely paid a living wage.[2] The earning of money, however, is incidental to professionalism, and not intrinsic as it is for business. Acting professionally, therefore, may be what individuals and organisations think they want but, in fact, to want this prevents the true aims of business from being achieved.

IDENTIFYING THE WORLD OF BUSINESS

In order to make sense of such assertions it will be necessary to discuss very carefully how terms like 'business' and 'profession' are used. What is meant by 'management' is perhaps the pivot for that discussion. This section will not attempt to define terms in any formal sense, but rather to illustrate how they are used, and to suggest how the writer would like to see them used. For the professions to use 'business' words and for business to use 'professional' words is misleading. When it is clear what is meant by the respective institutions, the road will be clear to see what role can be ascribed to ethics and what ethical behaviour might mean in the context of business.

Business or trade is concerned with producing what (the relevant) society needs or wants. In a market economy, this produce will be purchased by customers for money. An element of that money will be profit. Exactly what counts as profit, as opposed to overheads or the cost of production, is complicated but, for the purpose of this chapter, it will be taken to mean an amount of money given to an owner which would not be given to an employee. In other words, profit is taken to be unearned income. Traditionally, the object of business is profit.

It should be pointed out that the view of the professional put forward in this chapter rests on the motive both of the agent and the work. A change in the ownership of profit or the purpose to which profit is put cannot change business into a profession. Any difference would lie in the degree to which the business was held to be ethical.

Management is both the art and the tool of business. The job of management is to decide the aims and objectives of a particular business (the art) and to put them into effect (the tool). It will be the owners (or appointed agents, namely the directors in the case of a company) of business who practise the art, and the employed managers who are the tools. In neither case, though, are managers professionals in the sense that doctors or lawyers are. Theirs is a different job.

A customer is the purchaser of the produce of business. There is no duty of care, *per se*, on the part of business towards that customer. That is to say, the essence of the relationship is not based on care or the provision of service but on the supply of goods. Increased regard for quality and/or safety are understood here as springing from market forces or from government regulations. That business is conducted more 'altruistically' does not change the core relationship.

Before looking at the words associated with professionalism, let us consider how ethics can fit into the world of business. If the predominant aim of business is to make profit, then is an ethical business person someone who makes most profit? On this simple analysis the answer must certainly be 'yes'. If ethical business is to mean more than that, there must be other values in operation in business as well as the profit motive.

THE PROFESSIONS

What is the nature of a profession such that profit is not central to it? Daryl Koehn defines professionals in terms of the 'desires' or wants of their clients.[3] 'The professional is a person who provides service to a client. . . . [P]ersons become clients because they seek some good they lack and are unable to provide for themselves. The unhealthy, injured/accused, and sinful soul all want help in obtaining or recovering something they think desirable – health, a fair share, or spiritual wholeness respectively. . . . These desiring persons give professionals their being. Trusting that the minister, doctor, and lawyer will act on their behalf, . . . [they] enter into relations with unfamiliar professionals' (p. 58). Trust, rather than power, is regarded as crucial. In addition, Koehn says that a 'professional is an agent who freely makes a public promise to serve persons (e.g. the sick) who are distinguished by a specific desire for a particular good (e.g. health)' (p. 59).

Essential elements of the relationship are the professional's desire to do good for a client and to tailor the 'good' to the particular needs of the client. Good is defined here in ethical terms as being more or less health, health being the moral object of the relationship between, in this example, doctor and client.

But how different is this relationship from that subsisting between customer and supplier/manufacturer? Does not a customer have some want or desire that business can satisfy? Payment cannot be the key, for a client, either directly or indirectly, pays for the services of a professional just as the customer pays for goods bought from a manufacturer. Is the difference in the nature of what is purchased – services or goods? Certainly the increased number of groups in recent years[4] – insurance brokers, counsellors of various sorts, and even personnel and managers – claiming professional status is paralleled by the increase of the so-called service industries; but here the word service is used to distinguish them from manufacturing, and not because they are professional.

The personnel manager who learns to make staff feel valued and happy (though it may take five years, for example, to acquire such skills) is but one step removed from the means of production, the purpose of which is profit. The intention of the insurance broker or salesman is to make money from selling a policy, even though the insurance business involves highly complex and specialised information. Members of service industries can be *experts*, but they are not professionals.

THE VALUES OF BUSINESS

So, if business cannot be fitted into the 'good intentions' of the professions, how can ethical behaviour be made sense of? Defining the term 'professional' to include an intrinsic good intention, some moral aspect, in no way precludes business from having morality; it merely acknowledges that immoral business is as possible as moral business. Neither term necessarily indicates good business in terms of successful profit making. Immorality in a professional, on the other hand, necessarily involves 'being unprofessional' and thus does mean unsuccessful in terms of the task in hand. Business may decide, either by itself or under the influence of market forces (which affect profitability and are therefore at the heart of business ethics), that profit should not, as opposed to cannot, be made 'at any cost', without regard, for example, to the environment or human safety. It may be appropriate to consider that, whether or not the essential nature of business or professionalism may not change, particular values can change. Certainly the behavioural out-come of a value can vary from time to time: for example, our under-standing of marital fidelity differs in the light of changing attitudes to divorce.

What are the values of business? Aristotle[5] (*inter alia*) states that the aim [and value] of business is profit. As such, a good business is one where as much money as possible is made. 'Good' is not used here to mean virtuous, and only has meaning in terms of the most profit. To say to a businessperson that they are under a duty to pre-serve the environment as a businessperson is meaningless. The only appeal is that such a duty may or may not apply to *every* human being. In such circumstances it is up to the community at large to pass laws to control the freedom available in which to make profit. The 'most profit possible' will be construed accordingly. 'Good' business, however, will not have a different meaning, even though less profit is made or the environment is preserved.

Another value of business, either as well as profit or as an alter-native, could be to supply demand. 'Good' business would be busi-ness which fills demand most adequately. In this analysis there perhaps would be more room to negotiate that 'good' might include having regard for the environment, for example, as one might argue that supplying demand long-term would only be possible if raw materials were still available. There are a lot of variables, neverthe-less, in such an argument, because of difficulties in predicting future demand. 'Good' is not, however, to do with virtue here, but to do with having the continued ability to supply demand. To consider this, rather than profit, as the central value of business invites dis-cussion on whether the ownership of business is significant – for example, if business is state- or privately owned.

Is there virtue in supplying people's needs, rather than their wants? There might be. In other than voluntary organisations, sup-plying need is a value which is subordinate to the value of making profit. In nationalised industries, profit is not necessarily the prim-ary motive, but nevertheless the financial viability of the industry will be a condition of whether the industry survives without subsidy from some other source of national money. Even if we allow that some virtue might attach to the motive involved in nationalised industries, the virtue does not belong to the industry itself but to the nation, the government, or the electorate who commissions it. 'Good' work does not mean virtuous work in this context. As has already been said, the present classification is two-fold: it takes account of the intention of both agent and work. As such, a change in ownership of profit cannot convert business into something else; the fact that profit is spent on the purchase of health, for example, may affect the degree to which business is ethical, but it will not change its nature.

MANAGERS ARE NOT PROFESSIONALS

It will by now be clear why this writer thinks that managers are not professionals. Managers themselves, however, are at some pains to say that they *are*. In the Code of Conduct issued to its members by the Institute of Management[6] it is stated that:

Membership of a professional body implies that a duty of care is accepted in respect of those affected by the pursuit of professional activities.

Paragraph 1 of the Code, on p. 29, states:

A professional man or woman is one who justifiably claims to provide an expert service of value to society, and who accepts the duties . . . including . . . honouring the special trust reposed by clients, employers, colleagues, and the general public.

This is a reasonable description of what a professional does. What is not clear is how it can apply to managers. It is not a question of whether a manager performs his or her job well. The Code specifically prohibits abuse of power, for example, but that does not strike at the heart of being a professional but at being human. A manager does not choose *what* job is done, in the same way as a doctor chooses treatment to make a patient well, although the manager may have scope in deciding *how* the job is done. The job of a manager is to implement the requirement of a particular business: in other words, to persuade or procure other employees (including less senior managers) to obey (in accordance with their respective contracts of employment) the orders of the owners and/or directors of the business. That surely is a description of an act of selling. The expertise and skill involved in performing the act are not in dispute, but the framework of a professional relationship is absent. There is no client to whom a duty of care can be owed in the same way that a doctor owes a duty of care to a patient. In the sense that any member of society can be unwell, and thus is a potential patient or client, so it can be argued that a doctor offers some service of value to society and that there is thus some sort of relationship between the general public and the professional. How such a framework can fit with the work of a manager (however well, ethically or otherwise, that work is done) is hard to see.

A professional footballer certainly reaches heights of excellence and skill, but this is a different use of the word 'professional'. Managers have free claim to this use.

Airaksinen, in an analysis which excludes engineering (which he calls a pseudo-profession) from the professions,[7] classifies a profession as having an internal good. He finds the good – for example, health in the profession of medicine – to be a value which nobody could question. By contrast, he argues (p. 7) that building a bridge may or may not be good; and further, that the alleged internal values of engineering (public safety, health and welfare), while desirable, are incidental rather than intrinsic values. In the same way, 'being ethical' is incidental to business and management; it does not have sufficiently close a relationship to make either a profession.

THE ROLE OF THE IN-HOUSE PROFESSIONAL

In the majority of working relationships, the most important source of information about what is right and wrong conduct between the parties is the contract of employment, be it written, oral or construed by statute. The contract quite ably governs not only technicalities, like what should be done, when, by whom and for what remuneration, but also some moral tenets like obedience, loyalty and confidentiality. This is important, as the obedience or compliance with a legally enforceable provision should not be mistaken for moral intent. Likewise, a company complying with legally enforceable safety regulations may or may not be ethical. Any morality on the part of the company must exist outside or in excess of the legal requirement. When the employee is also a professional, there are factors to consider which the contract cannot adequately accommodate. The employed professional is as subject to the guidance and governance of his or her professional body as if they were self-employed. Making such adherence a term of the contract merely further confuses a situation where there will always be potential conflict of interest and/or divided loyalty. The absence of easy answers to the questions 'Who is the client and who the advisor? Who is master and who servant? Who should obey whose command?', clearly illustrates the difficult nature of such a relationship.

THE GP FUNDHOLDER – BUSINESSPERSON OR PROFESSIONAL?

Probably one of the most complex manifestations of a professional structure is the hospital. It is a matter of degree and actuality in each particular case whether a hospital manager, for example, albeit a qualified doctor, has crossed over into business. The essential motive behind the existence of a hospital, however, has traditionally been to promote health. This is a professional motive.

If intention is the deciding factor, though, a profit motive behind a hospital's existence carries it out of the professional and into the business sector. Increasingly, even in former National Health establishments, this would seem to be the case.

The term 'GP Fundholder' is defined by the NHS and Community Care Act 1990, and means a doctors' practice that is owned and run by the doctors and not funded directly or otherwise by a health authority or other statutory body.[8] The change in ownership of a doctors' practice does not necessarily have an effect on the practice's professionalism. A solicitors' practice, for example, is not prevented from being professional because it is not government owned, so why should this new sort of doctor's practice cause concern? Is there concern? Is it health, and the structure and dispensation of health, that makes the fundholding GP's position different from that of the lawyer? Concern in this instance would seem not to be about ownership but about the way health services are now to be sold. Under the scheme, patients do not pay the doctor direct but via a 'state sorting house', namely, the former health authority. Roughly speaking, a doctor is given a *per capita* allowance for the patients on his or her list. If some patients need more expensive treatment than others, no additional monies are paid, but there is a sort of 'averaging out'. Thus the new system can be seen as halfway to an open market. The way the financing is structured, however, invites the doctor to pay more attention to the cost of treatment than to what is the best treatment for a particular patient. The professional practice is being manoeuvred (by government) towards behaving like a business, concerning itself more with profit and/or supply and demand than with health. In comparison, the payment of solicitors in practice is structured rather differently.[9] Some clients pay directly from their own funds. Those who are unable to pay receive assistance from the Legal Aid Fund. Help is given largely according to the means of the client, not the nature of the legal help required. As such, the impact on professional discretion arguably is reduced, as there is a much less obvious relationship between income and professional advice. This difference is reinforced in the law because there are usually two 'sides', with two sets of lawyers involved. In medicine, however, there is one patient and one doctor (or one 'set' of doctors).

Consistent with the basis upon which business management is excluded from professionalism, this new emphasis in the structure of a GP Fundholding practice, whereby there are finite resources to be distributed among unidentified patients, is in danger of taking doctors away from the essence of professionalism. They are no longer free to assess the client's or patient's needs first and then to work out what is required. Instead, the temptation is for doctors to pre-select patients or groups of patients, or worse still, further to depersonalise the patients by precluding types of complaint, namely those which are the most expensive to treat. This commercialisation of medicine, if taken to the extreme, has the ability to de-professionalise health services. Other professionals following a similar route, whereby the selection and servicing of clients is changed, would likewise jeopardise their own professionalism.

THE WAY FORWARD IS THE WAY BACK

The respective motives of professions and business are complementary but opposite. The professional, having listened to the particular circumstances of the client, from the stock of knowledge and possible solutions available tries to tailor a 'product' that will be good for the client. On the other hand, business tries to persuade the customer to minimise any peculiarities and to realise that what is 'good' for him or her is the very product that is on sale. Business may carry out market research in order to find out what most customers think will be good for them, but the motive is to make a product that has a general appeal and then to sell as many of them as possible. The motive is profit for itself. Similar attempts by professionals to 'standardise' their 'product', rather than to enhance their essential nature which is to provide an individual service, in fact diminishes their effectiveness *qua* professionals. Such practices give them the pretended appearance of business.

In recent times the distinction between the professions and business has become confused. Business, particularly its managers, has tried to assume professional status.[10] Professional practice and practices have pressed for greater commercialisation. It has been argued that neither phenomenon can retain its special character by moving towards the other.

What also emerges is that there are two aspects to the intention which is at the heart of how professionalism and business have been defined: that is, the intention of the agent and that of the work must be of the same nature, namely that a profession must have an integral good value and business must have profit as its main focus. If business genuinely seeks to improve its ethical image, then it must change its ways within its own values. Pretending to be professional will do nothing of substance: indeed, establishing its morality upon such false foundations can only worsen the image of business and plunge it further into hypocrisy. Likewise, professionals must retain and nourish their essential nature rather than try to be 'trendy' and court a business image.

NOTES

1 Institute of Management (1994) 'The Manager as a Professional', *Business Review*, 3(1), pp. 29–47.

2 General Synod of the Church of England (1994) *Church Commissioners as the Central Stipend Authority: The 22nd Report*, London: General Synod of the Church of England. Some licence has been taken in this statement because, although, in monetary terms, the clergyman's salary is below average, the whole remuneration package is probably about the male average. It is, however, far below what a successful tax lawyer would get.

3 Koehn, D. (1994) *The Ground of Professional Ethics*, London: Routledge.

4 Harris, N. (1989) *Professional Codes of Conduct in the UK: A Directory*, London: Mansell.

5 Thomson, J. A. K. (1953) *The Ethics of Aristotle*, London: Penguin Books.

6 Institute of Management, 'The Manager as a Professional', p. 28.

7 Airaksinen, T. (1994) 'Service and Science in Professional Life', in Chadwick, Ruth (ed.), *Ethics and the Professions*, Aldershot: Avebury, pp. 1–13.

8 Pritchard, Jane (1994) 'Applied Ethics and Managing Change in the Health Field', in Henry, C. (ed.) *Professional Ethics and Organisational Change*, London: Edward Arnold, pp.16–30.

9 The Legal Aid system is currently under review. Some proposals would bring funding more into line with that of health services.

10 Institute of Management, 'The Manager as a Professional'. For example, the Institute of Management has issued a *Code of Conduct and Guides to Professional Management Practice*, which was revised in September 1991.

8

CODES OF ETHICS
Some uses and abuses
Iain Munro

INTRODUCTION

It is no doubt true that a company's reputation is of fundamental importance in an age of increasing consumer awareness. Also, there is a great deal of evidence to show that people are becoming increasingly sensitive to the moral issues of everyday business.[1] One of the clearest symptoms of this concern has been the recent proliferation of company codes of ethics, particularly in the UK and the US.

Given this recent interest in codes of ethics, it will prove fruitful to examine how they are used in practice and the kinds of problems that they can be used to address. This chapter will attempt to bring to the surface some of the most pressing issues which are involved when implementing such codes, including both moral and the more pragmatic concerns. First, codes will be examined in terms of their various benefits, such as their effects on public relations and their role in putting ethical concerns on the business agenda. Second, the process of implementing such codes will be discussed, with a particular focus on who is involved in their formulation and how they might reasonably be enforced. The final part of this chapter will show that there are many kinds of problems for which codes are not applicable, with particular reference to the cultural and political dimensions of the organisation.

THE BENEFITS OF A CODE

Benefits to the organisation: public relations

Probably the most obvious use of a company code of ethics is as part of a public relations exercise. It is quite clear that some companies, such as the Cooperative Bank and The Body Shop, have promoted their codes of ethics to great effect. These companies have attempted to appeal to the moral sensibilities of consumers as part of their overall marketing strategy. Indeed, one company has recently advertised on television that 'We care because you do'.

However, many companies which have adopted their own ethical policies have been rather less successful in this regard. Evidence suggests that companies tend to restrict their codes to top managers and shareholders, and rarely distribute them to outside interest groups.[2] In fact, many companies have failed to allay the fears of their critics despite having adopted ethical policies to justify their activities. This is most apparent in cases where companies have suffered boycotts of their products, such as the oil giants, EXXON and Shell, which continue to be severely criticised for their environmental record, and the pharmaceutical company, Boots, which has failed to satisfy the demands of animal rights pressure groups.

So it would appear that many companies have not fully exploited the public relations potential of their ethical codes. One way of tapping this potential may be through using the code as part of an overall marketing strategy. Also, pressure groups need not be seen in an entirely hostile light and can provide valuable information on many controversial aspects of business practice. Many UK companies already sponsor the initiatives of popular environmental pressure groups, such as Friends of the Earth and the World Wide Fund for Nature.[3] The Cooperative Bank even supports its ethical policies with research prepared by the human rights group Amnesty International.

Of course, to some extent conflicts will be unavoidable where businesses operate in areas of social controversy. Sir Adrian Cadbury has pointed out that managers must weigh up a whole range of interests, whereas pressure groups have the privilege of being somewhat more single-minded in pursuit of their objectives.[4] However, it could be objected that many pressure groups have emerged in the first place due to the overwhelming imbalance in the priorities of the business community. This brings us to a question that is fundamental to business ethics, that is, just what are the social responsibilities of business?

Benefits to the stakeholders: social responsibilities

A host of burning social issues has been raised in the texts of UK company codes of ethics; those most commonly mentioned include environmental issues, health and safety, community relations, equal opportunities, political activities, fair pay, bribery, the misuse of information and the integrity of employees.[5] This list is by no means exhaustive. In their codes of ethics many companies have explicitly recognised a very broad range of stakeholder interests, including responsibilities to customers, suppliers, employees, shareholders, the local community and the environment. Indeed, it is of some significance that shareholders are one of the least mentioned interest groups in the texts of these codes. This would seem to indicate a significant difference to the traditional capitalist ethic where a firm's responsibilities were confined to the basic contractual obligations to shareholders.

One of the earliest academic discussions of the social responsibilities of business was given by the Nobel Laureate Milton Friedman, who proposed that the only social responsibility of business was to increase profits.[6] However, even Friedman felt compelled to add a few conditions to this principle, such as that people should obey the law and respect the basic ethical customs of society. The force of Friedman's argument is at its weakest here, since he does not consider that social values can change or that they can come into conflict. For instance, it is not clear from this view whether we are to carry on gobbling up the world's resources at an extravagant rate, or whether it would be more appropriate to cultivate an environmental ethic which is more sensitive to the effects of rapid changes in technology and production.

Generally speaking, Friedman's is the predominant view to be found in company mission statements and codes of ethics. However, the precise interpretation of this minimalist philosophy varies significantly from company to company. The most common view reflected in UK company codes is that, by making profits, the common good will necessarily follow, although some companies are slightly less optimistic, suggesting that profits are necessary if other social responsibilities are to be fulfilled.[7] These 'other' social responsibilities include projects such as increased community involvement and the adoption of environmental initiatives – policies which many successful companies have already adopted. Although these are not strictly profit maximising initiatives, many important long-term benefits may be derived from them, such as a good reputation, a healthier working environment, and good community relations.

From the above analysis it appears that company codes can be developed to address a wide range of issues, and that some companies have already perceived the potential of their ethical codes. But many aspects of code development have not yet been covered, particularly as regards their enforcement.

PROCEDURES FOR IMPLEMENTATION

Formulation and commitment

In practice, company codes of ethics have been developed and enforced by a fairly select band of people, notably the top management of companies.[8] The dissemination of these codes tends to be restricted to the shareholders and the upper echelons of the corporate ladder. By excluding the views of so many employees from the formulation process, it is likely that these people will feel little commitment to their company's code. Indeed, since anyone is quite capable of pointing out cases of misconduct, it would seem wise to represent the interests of all employees in code formulation and enforcement. This can be said on both moral and practical grounds.

On moral grounds, it is difficult to see why the views of managers should be included in a code when the views of other employees are excluded. Company codes of conduct have been criticised for containing an excessive bias towards the interests of their enforcers, both in the US and the UK.[9] Enforcing a code of ethics presents us with some rather vexing problems, at the heart of which is the age-old question, 'Who shall guard the guardians?' (Juvenal's *Satires*). To navigate this knotty problem, one might begin by involving representatives from different parts of the organisation in the formulation and enforcement of its ethical code, rather than leaving it to a well intentioned managerial elite. If implemented in this way, a code could provide a point of reference to encourage an environment in which ethical concerns may be dealt with in an open and candid manner. There is a strong moral argument that a person's interests cannot be adequately represented unless they are given voice.[10]

Greater participation in the formulation and enforcement of codes also has many practical advantages. For one thing, codes that are implemented in this way will be far less open to the criticism that they are mere window-dressing, devoid of any ethical content. Many of the most successful ethical policies in operation today are highly participatory in nature, such as organised money-raising events for charity and the secondment of professionals to community projects. And, as noted earlier, many indirect benefits, such as increased employee morale and good community relations, can be derived from these kinds of ethical policies.

Enforcement and discipline

Another way in which commitment towards a code may be generated is by backing it with a list of suitable sanctions. While this approach has been strongly recommended within the academic literature, companies seem reluctant to employ such severe measures in practice.[11] A large number of codes are not specific enough to permit enforcement of this kind. This could be a sign that managers do not think they have the right to enforce moral standards on their employees in this way, although it may also signal a lack of commitment to ethical standards in general. Whatever the case, some benefit might be gained by exploring some alternative avenues for the enforcement of codes, such as the idea of discipline without punishment.[12]

The non-punitive approach to discipline is far more subtle than traditional punitive measures. When violations of company policy occur, the appropriate enforcement officer should meet privately with the offending employee to discuss the problem informally. This should not involve the threat of punishment, but should be a sincere attempt to understand the offender's position. If the problem persists, the next step would be to issue a written reminder. Eventually, the offender may have to be put on paid suspension to consider the situation. In the non-punitive approach to discipline, the idea is to gain the offender's agreement to change. The aim of this approach to enforcement is to minimise the stigmatisation of the offender, and to reduce possible feelings of injustice and resentment which result from the threat of punishment.

This non-punitive approach to discipline may be considered to be a far more humanist approach to enforcing standards of good conduct than simply using the threat of sanctions. In practice, there does seems to be some persuasive evidence to suggest that this approach yields many other benefits, such as reductions in employee turnover, disciplinary incidents and grievances.[13] One caveat concerning the approach is that it may serve to extend the influence of management over the moral choices of other employees. Therefore, the ethical concerns of employees must be given a forum for debate, in order to avoid the danger that managers might be cast unwarily in the role of moral experts. Now that some of the most difficult fundamental problems concerning code implementation have been outlined, it will become clearer where their limitations lie.

THE LIMITATIONS OF A CODE

The priorities and dilemmas of business

Although company codes may be used to address a number of important moral issues in business, it should be clear that there are many problems for which they will be entirely inapplicable. To begin with, codes of ethics may be very effective in setting the agenda for a company, but less so in prioritising particular issues. This is certainly true in practice, where priorities are usually left unclear in the texts of the codes.[14] Formulating a code to cover all the various possibilities is likely to prove a somewhat fruitless task, since it may be very difficult to find clear-cut rules which are applicable in all situations. The very nature of moral dilemmas is that they arise from the existing norms of behaviour, which sometimes demand contradictory things of a person. A classic example of this has been related by Sartre, who told of an experience in the Second World War when one of his pupils approached him with a painful dilemma. The story he related was of a young man living alone with his mother, who had already lost one son in action and was estranged from her husband. The remaining son felt torn between looking after his mother and going to fight for the Free French Forces based in England; he could not fulfil one duty without neglecting the other, and in this case there was nothing to tell him which way to decide except his own conscience. Although norms and values existed to frame this situation, they demanded contradictory actions. In fact, there is plenty of evidence to suggest that people frequently encounter such dilemmas as part of their everyday working lives.[15] In this regard, many existing codes can be criticised, since they do not allow for the existence of any real dilemmas and simplistically recommend that employees should always resolve conflicts in favour of the company;[16] the moral content of such statements is at best contentious.

In such situations, obedience cannot be considered to be a virtue, instead, one must think through the problem and be sensitive to the weight of the interests at stake. Of course, the nature of a dilemma is that one may be forced to make a decision either way without knowing which course is best. Sartre observed that, when we are faced with a dilemma, no one can make the choice for us, since there are no experts in moral matters.[17] To do otherwise, and depend on the advice of another, would be to commit an act of bad faith, abrogating one's responsibility.

Action and context

Another limitation of company codes of ethics is that they tend to focus attention upon the misconduct of isolated individuals, and are not much concerned with how moral problems arise in the first place. Ethical codes simply cannot capture the complexities involved in modern business life. This is only too clear in the case of recent corporate disasters, where the official inquiries have often found it extremely difficult to blame any particular individuals – to do so would be to miss the point.[18] Anthony Hidden, the QC who investigated the Clapham Junction rail accident, found that negligent working practices were not confined to a few isolated individuals but were widespread throughout the culture of British Rail. Like so many other corporate disasters, it was an accident waiting to happen.[19]

The fact is that there may be little motivation to obey official standards when there are far more immediate pressures to disregard them. The official rules of an organisation do little to modify attitudes towards work, although they are often used as bargaining chips in negotiations between rival factions within an organisation.[20] So the effect of the official rules is not only to mitigate some tensions, but to conceal others and allow them to persist. Therefore, in practice, rules often do not remove the problems that they are designed to deal with.

BUILDING ON A CODE OF ETHICS: A FORUM FOR MORAL DIALOGUE

To expose any differences between the rhetoric and the reality of codes, ethical concerns must be permitted to arise at any level of decision-making within an organisation. Single-line communication through one's supervisor or manager is unlikely to improve things, since many moral concerns may be directly related to the nature of this relationship and, in any case, it would seem to imply that moral superiority is in some way associated with bureaucratic seniority.

One way to address such problems is by the initiation of a forum for debate within organisations, through which the political barriers to change may be overcome.[21] A dialogical approach to business ethics can be used to enrich our working lives in a number of ways. There is a strong moral argument that the views of others cannot be adequately considered without engaging in a moral discourse, where anyone should be able to challenge the validity of an argument, and the participants should not use their official power in an attempt to side-step such reasonable questions. If ethical concerns can be aired freely within an organisation, this may go some way to reducing the 'moral stress' that many people already feel.[22] This approach has also been recommended to avert corporate disasters before they have a chance to develop.[23]

CONCLUSIONS

Ethical codes of practice can be adopted by companies to set out what they deem to be their social responsibilities, and to establish standards of good conduct for their employees. These codes may have many advantages in terms of both public relations and creating an environment in which the ethical concerns of employees can be raised openly. Many difficult questions may be faced when adopting a code, such as who should be involved, what areas should the code cover and how should it be enforced? In an attempt to account for the moral and practical problems which may be involved, it may be productive to emphasise the participatory nature of code implementation, both in its formulation and its enforcement. On the moral level, the participation of representatives spanning the corporate hierarchy may overcome some of the ideological problems involved in code implementation, and on the practical level, it may generate much more commitment from the employees.

However, even the best-worked code will still be inapplicable to a wide range of moral concerns in business. For one thing, codes are almost useless to individual employees who are faced with their own particular dilemmas. Also, codes cannot be used to address the deeper social currents which give rise to many of the moral problems in modern-day business. In such cases, it is essential that a moral debate ensues to bring to the surface the knotty issues and dilemmas that may be involved.

NOTES

1 Brenner, S. and Molander, E. (1977) 'Is the Ethics of Business Changing?', *Harvard Business Review*, 55(1), pp. 57–71; Waters, J., Bird, F. and Chant, P. (1986) 'Everyday Moral Issues Experienced by Managers', *Journal of Business Ethics*, 5(5), pp. 373–84; Forrester, Susan (1990) *Business and Environmental Groups – a natural partnership?*, London: The Directory of Social Change.

2 Melrose-Woodman, J. and Kverndal, I. (1976) *Towards Social Responsibility: Company Codes of Ethics and Practice*, Management Survey Report No. 28, Corby: British Institute of Management; Schlegelmich, B. and Houston, J. (1988) *Corporate Codes of Ethics in Large U.K Companies: An Empirical Investigation of Use, Content and Attitudes, Working Paper Series*, University of Edinburgh; Munro, I. (1995) *Moral Regulation in Business: An Investigation into Corporate Codes of Ethics*, PhD thesis, University of Hull.

3 Forrester, *Business and Environmental Groups*.

4 Cadbury, Sir A. (1987) 'Ethical Managers Make their Own Rules'. *Harvard Business Review*, 65(5), pp. 69–75.

5 Munro, *Moral Regulation in Business*.

6 Friedman, M. (1970) 'The Social Responsibility of Business is to Increase its Profits', *New York Times Magazine*, 13 September.

7 Munro, *Moral Regulation in Business*.

8 Melrose-Woodman and Kverndal, *Towards Social Responsibility*; Schlegelmich and Houston, *Corporate Codes of Ethics in Large U.K. Companies*; Munro, *Moral Regulation in Business*.

9 Cressey, D. and Moore, C. (1983) 'Managerial Values and Corporate Codes of Ethics', *California Management Review*, 25(4), pp. 53–77; see also Munro, *Moral Regulation in Business*.

10 Kant, I. (1785) *The Moral Law*, trans. H. J. Paton, London: Hutchinson; Habermas, J. (1990) *Moral Consciousness and Communicative Action*, Oxford: Blackwell.

11 Berenbeim, R. (1992) *Corporate Ethics Practice*, New York: The Conference Board; see also Munro, *Moral Regulation in Business*.

12 Huberman, J. (1964) 'Discipline Without Punishment', *Harvard Business Review*, 42(4), pp. 62–7.

13 Huberman, J. (1975) 'Discipline Without Punishment Lives', *Harvard Business Review*, 53(4), pp. 6–8; Campbell, D., Fleming, R. and Grote,

R. (1985) 'Discipline without punishment – at last', *Harvard Business Review*, 63(4), pp. 162–78.

14 Hosmer, L. (1987) *The Ethics of Management*, Homewood, Ill.: Irwin.

15 Brenner and Molander, 'Is the Ethics of Business Changing?'; Waters *et al.*, 'Everyday Moral Issues Experienced by Managers'.

16 Munro, *Moral Regulation in Business*.

17 Sartre, J.-P. (1956) *Being and Nothingness*, New York: Philosophical Library.

18 Hidden, A. (1989) *An Investigation into the Clapham Junction railway accident*, London: HMSO; Boyd, C. (1989) *Ethical Issues Arising from the Zeebrugge Car Ferry Disaster*, unpublished paper, University of Toronto.

19 Jones, T. (1988) *Corporate Killing: Bhopals Will Happen*, London: Free Association.

20 Gouldner, A. (1954) *Patterns of Industrial Bureaucracy*, New York: The Free Press.

21 Payne, S. (1991) 'A proposal for Corporate Ethical Reform: The Ethical Dialogue Group', *The Business and Professional Ethics Journal*, 10(1), pp. 67–88; Bowen, M. and Power, F. (1993) 'The Moral Manager: Communicative Ethics and the *EXXON Valdez* Disaster', *Business Ethics Quarterly*, 3(2), pp. 97–116.

22 Waters *et al.*, 'Everyday Moral Issues Experienced by Managers'.

23 Bowen and Power, 'The Moral Manager'.

9

WHISTLEBLOWING AND ITS ALTERNATIVES

Angela Peek

INTRODUCTION

Around 90 per cent of UK managers claim that they would speak out on ethical issues such as financial misconduct, treatment of employees and control of information, if they witnessed misconduct in these areas in their organisations.[1] Would these good intentions be put into practice in a real life scenario? Sadly, the experiences of those employees who do put words into action and become 'whistle-blowers' give little encouragement to the ethical individual. Charles Robertson, who blew the whistle on false declarations to the Inland Revenue at Guardian Royal Exchange, describes the personal consequences of his decision to blow the whistle thus: 'I applied for getting on for forty jobs, and in that time I had only one interview, which did not result in a job offer . . . companies didn't want me, I was not acceptable. . . . When I was dismissed, the bottom fell out of my world really. . . . I'd thrown my career away.'[2]

For those who follow the dictates of their conscience, rather than those of their employer, and speak out over malpractice, is such a sorry result inevitable? A survey in the US of eighty-seven individuals who had blown the whistle on corruption, abuse, waste, fraud, and safety violations, after trying to raise the matter with someone in the organisation, found that retaliation resulted for all but one of them: most lost their jobs, 17 per cent lost their homes, 15 per cent were divorced and 10 per cent attempted suicide; some suffered loss of faith in themselves, in others, in government and in the judicial system.[3]

In the UK, many cases still come to light where individuals who were aware of some impropriety did not speak out. Systematic mental and physical abuse in mental homes in the north-west of

England, a supervisor knowing about the loose wiring that was a crucial factor in the Clapham train crash, workers afraid to speak out prior to the Piper Alpha explosion – these examples show that those who knew either tried to speak out at the workplace and were victimised and afraid to carry on, or said nothing for fear of rocking the boat or losing their jobs. What are the options for the potential whistleblower, and can the typical consequences described above be avoided?

WHAT IS A WHISTLEBLOWER?

There is a wide variety of definitions of what constitutes a whistleblower. For our purposes, a working definition is: 'An employee or ex-employee of an organisation, who discloses information about serious malpractice by that organisation, not otherwise known or visible, where the disclosure is made in the reasonable belief that there is malpractice, and the disclosure is made in good faith, without malice, and may be in the public interest'.

Self-appointed spies or company troublemakers whistleblowers are not. Public Concern At Work, the UK charity set up to advise would-be whistleblowers, received over 1500 enquiries in its first year of operation. The five largest sources of concern were local government (73), health services (70), education (46), charities (38) and care facilities (35). Of the 386 public concerns that fell within its remit, 187 related to financial malpractice, 83 to workplace safety, 67 to public safety and 25 to child or patient abuse.[4] The US survey described above found a typical whistleblower to be a married man with children, around 40 years old, employed by the company for seven years on average, who blew the whistle only after trying to raise the alarm internally. Another survey pointed to the individuals' firm belief in the company and their long histories of successful employment. They were 'convinced that if they took a grievance to superiors, there would be an appropriate response. This naïvety led them into a series of damaging traps . . . their earlier service and dedication provided them with little protection against charges of undermining organizational morale and effectiveness.'[5]

A DIFFICULT ENVIRONMENT

To repeat, whistleblowers are not troublemakers. They represent a genuine and necessary public and workplace safety-net. Vigilant employees must be able to come forward and report cases of mal-practice, fraud, safety violations, etc., both for the public's sake, and for the sake of the company wishing to maintain its public image and do the right thing. The business scandals of recent years sug-gest that it is important to protect the public and employees from sharp practice. Cases such as the Maxwell pension fund scandal and the collapse of BCCI, etc., indicate that, in the minds of some busi-ness leaders, the law is to be circumvented, and loopholes found. However, this does not occur simply at the top of organisations, although certain pressures may emanate from that source. Middle management may be guilty of flouting the law and cutting corners, with the perceived dictates of senior management and the need to get the job done at any cost overcoming regard for employee and public safety. Further, instances such as the thirteen-year reign of terror by Frank Beck in Leicestershire childrens' homes show how serious malpractice can remain undetected and hidden at multiple levels.

The trend in modern business is towards larger and more decen-tralised organisations, that boast flatter structures and greater devo-lution of power and responsibility. At the other end of the scale, small businesses are working in an increasingly competitive environ-ment and may find themselves under increasing pressure to behave unethically or cut corners – in such companies, vigilant employees may find themselves highly vulnerable. Rather than legislate, the preferred way forward has been to deregulate. The employers have been identified as the vehicle for vigilance, facing increased penalties when they fail in this duty. But the abuses continue apace. The role of individual employees has been ignored in this equation, yet their vigilance represents a key factor in regulating the practice of busi-ness within private and public sector organisations.

The most visible public response to the need for increased cor-porate governance has been the Cadbury Working Group, which has been responsible for implementing the findings of the UK's Committee on the Financial Aspects of Corporate Governance (the Cadbury Committee). The Committee considered it 'good practice for boards to draw up codes of ethics', but they were not felt impor-tant enough to be included in their recommended *Code of Best Practice.*

THE LAW

How does the law protect the genuine whistleblower, acting in good faith?[6] Employment law imposes on the employee duties of confidentiality and fidelity to the employer during the currency of an employment relationship. This generally prevents a disclosure which could embarrass or harm the employer. The consequences of this are far-reaching for the whistleblower. As employees must not disclose their employer's confidential information, the disclosure of anything that the employer describes as 'confidential', even if this is evidence of wrongdoing, then makes an employee in breach of this duty. Employees are also under a general duty not to act in a manner which is calculated or likely to destroy the 'mutual trust and confidence' on which the employment relationship is based.

Under common law, the unauthorised dissemination of information may have a 'just cause' defence, should the disclosure be in the public interest and to an appropriate recipient. The defence that a disclosure was made 'in the public interest' will be weighed by the court against the seriousness of the disclosed wrongdoing, the good faith of the employee in disclosing the information, to whom the information was disclosed, and how it was come by. However, the courts cannot be relied upon to accept such a 'public interest' defence, and it often represents an onerous burden of proof for the whistleblower. While this defence applies to a disclosure that reveals a crime, fraud or corruption, also covered are disclosures of matters of 'grave public concern', regardless of whether any wrongdoing by the employer has occurred. However, the precise definition of matters of 'grave public concern' remains uncertain.

On the side of the whistleblower, there are some duties that the employer owes the employee, but these tend to be less clearly defined and not so easily enforceable. The Employment Protection (Consolidation) Act of 1978 gives employees the right to a written statement of certain particulars of employment, minimum notice periods, and procedures for dismissal which include written warnings and reasons for dismissal in writing. Rights are established against unfair dismissal, and protection is given against victimisation short of dismissal for trade union membership. The Employment Acts of 1982 and 1985 set out basic claims for compensation of loss in unfair dismissal claims; also available is a 'special award' where the employee applies for reinstatement or re-engagement and interim financial relief pending hearing.

Working against this protection are: the setting of the maximum award in favour of the employee at £11,000 (the average award is £2200) – this is little disincentive to an unscrupulous employer; and the two-year qualification period required for its coverage.[7]

The Race Relations Act and the Sex Discrimination Act are examples of the few laws that could protect employees who disclose specific types of information to certain recipients. Employees should be protected against victimisation if they report discrimination on the grounds of race or sex. Unfortunately, these Acts have been the subject of both highly restrictive and ambiguous interpretation, significantly reducing the chances of success in these types of cases. Health and safety laws and regulations allow some protection to employees with a health and safety brief who report concerns of a health and safety nature. Section 57A of the Employment Protection (Consolidation) Act of 1978 protects to some extent designated health and safety representatives in the performance of their health and safety functions. For other employees, protection exists where they attempt to raise health and safety concerns with their employer. There is a requirement that they leave or propose to leave the workplace where the serious and imminent risk to health and safety exists, and also that they take action to protect themselves from such risk. A right not to be subjected to detriment by the employer in these circumstances is given under section 22A, but these two sections are not applicable to health and safety issues which affect the public at large.

Industrial tribunals are a common first port of call in any case of a contractual claim against an employer relating to unfair dismissal, wrongful dismissal or constructive dismissal. While there is no qualification period to seek redress here, industrial tribunals are not generally able to award compensation (the maximum award is £25,000) to reflect what has been lost, should they find in a whistleblower's favour. Reinstatement, which is rarely ordered by a tribunal, cannot actually be enforced, and may not always be personally desirable for the whistleblower, thus any employee acting out of the purest of intentions to right a perceived wrong cannot insist or may not want to be taken back into employment and can end up out of a job, out of pocket and with a bleak future. Not only that, but an employer is free to counter-claim in this scenario, and a whistleblowing individual can be sued for breach of confidence by an organisation seeking damages.

Protection for whistleblowers is currently (1995/6) being pursued in the House of Commons via the *Public Interest Disclosure Bill*.[8] This would give new rights to whistleblowers, including the ability to claim compensation for stress and loss of earnings, and to obtain injunctions to stop threats of punishment. There would also be safeguards for the employer; whistleblowers would only get protection if they disclosed information which was accurate, in good faith, not subject to monetary reward, and have previously exhausted all channels to take the matter up internally. But until such a Bill is passed, potential whistleblowers will have to depend on the less-than-adequate legal protection outlined here.

CODES OF CONDUCT

A code represents an important vehicle for raising and resolving ethical issues within the workplace. But it must be properly implemented – a code of ethics or code of conduct demands that the employer allows itself to be scrutinised by its employees – rhetoric must translate into a clearly set-out reality. It prevents the need for highly damaging external whistleblowing, and allows the public greater assurance that they won't one day find themselves suffering the fallout of unaccountable and dubious business decision making, through encouraging and empowering employees in the drive for ethical vigilance.

A code allows the company to deal with a 'mistaken' whistleblower, or a company troublemaker with a vindictive or frivolous motive for raising a concern, in a rational way. Those with genuine concerns, on the other hand, can have the issue properly addressed within the company. Codes vary in their effectiveness and reach. They should be agreed between employer and employee and then widely publicised, both within the organisation and outside, with every worker confident in their duty to uphold them. Training must reinforce the important process of defining, reviewing and upholding standards. From new inductees to directors, the company's standards should be explained through training, with their effectiveness regularly reviewed. Responding to employee concerns should be promoted, as Winfield[9] points out, not as part of the grievance procedure, but rather as part of quality enhancement. Most codes set guiding principles for the organisation aimed at preventing unlawful or unprofessional behaviour, as well as covering specific areas that refer to operating standards – for example on buying policies, safety, and environmental responsibilities. Company standards and objectives should be clearly defined, the guidelines on correct behaviour should be unambiguous. Procedures for raising concerns should be specific and clearly understood, and recourse to an independent third party in the event of non-resolution of the issue not in doubt. A concern raised seriously and ethically should be dealt with in the same way. Employees must feel fully confident that reprisals will not greet efforts made in good faith to uphold standards; quite the opposite – individuals whose efforts benefit the company should be rewarded.

EXTERNAL HELP

Where can concerned individuals turn to, outside of their immediate organisation, for possible help?

Professional associations   Membership of a professional body generally involves adherence to a professional code of practice, established in accordance with definite priorities, deviance from which can result in the loss of professional status. It could be expected, therefore, that an electrical engineer being asked to contravene his or her institute's code on safety issues should find unequivocal support from this source. Such support can vary considerably, but should be carefully followed up if it is available.

Regulatory bodies   Generally, there seems to be little clear guidance from the regulatory bodies, from whom rhetoric may be plentiful, but where support in reality can be thin on the ground. For example, the Department of Energy made available to workers on North Sea oil rigs a poster which read 'Your responsibility does not end when you leave this installation. If you are still dissatisfied with a safety matter when you return to shore, you should then contact the Department of Energy Inspector. . . . Your anonymity will be respected.' Oil rig worker Vaughan Mitchell made just such a report and was sacked. The DE refused to help him in his action against his employer, claiming that the inquiry results he required, which found the company guilty of unsafe practices, were 'confidential'.

Trade unions   The unions vary in their response to individuals wishing to report malpractice, and their power may not always extend far enough to support an individual fully. Hotlines and support are available, and publicised by some. For unions wishing to re-establish themselves, or who are looking for key areas to be addressed in the future, carefully examining the support and advice given to potential whistleblowers could and should be a key development opportunity.

Member of Parliament/pressure group/the media   A relevant pressure group, a Member of Parliament with a particular concern in the area upon which you wish to blow the whistle, or a campaigning news journalist or newspaper, may appear to be a source of support but, as with all outside agencies, there are a number of difficulties inherent in this approach. MPs, pressure groups and newspapers all deal with a large amount of correspondence and lobbying from 'worthy' causes on a daily basis; naturally this limits the whistleblower's chances of receiving the individual attention, hearing and action that is sought. Additionally, the decisions of such individuals and agencies about whether to take up a case may be determined by priorities that have nothing to do with the individual whistleblower's circumstances and concern. The concern may be taken up in the context of a wider agenda aimed at achieving a different end, with the result that the genuine concern of the whistleblower is jeopardised by the interests of an external agency.

A whistleblower is especially at risk if they approach the press to publicise a concern in the circumstance where internal channels have not been tried first. The courts, in such a case, would not take a kind view of such disclosure. If, exceptionally, media disclosure appears justified, the suspicions must be reasonably grounded. But disclosure to an inappropriate recipient may mean the genuine whistleblower who felt there was nowhere else to turn loses protection, whatever the circumstances.

WHISTLEBLOWER'S CHECKLIST

The path of the whistleblower is strewn with difficulties, and no certainty of success. Much thought should be given to the alternatives to blowing the whistle. Winfield[10] lists some possible alternatives for a potential whistleblower to consider:

• simply turn a blind eye and continue as normal
• try raising the concern within the organisation and hope for a successful outcome

- go outside of the company while still in its employ to blow the whistle, while attempting to maintain anonymity
- blow the whistle in the full knowledge of the employer while still employed, and take the consequences of its disapproval
- resign and say nothing; or
- resign and then blow the whistle

Before making this decision, Winfield suggests considering the following *Whistleblower's Checklist*:[11]

Examine the facts

1 Ask yourself if the practice is clearly illegal or potentially dangerous, or if it is simply questionable business policy. Is the public interest really at stake?
2 Be realistic about the potential human damage caused by blowing the whistle – damage to the company, its shareholders, its clients, your colleagues. Be realistic about what you are likely to achieve.
3 Be optimistic but also be prepared to lose, to be rejected by colleagues and friends and probably to see your family suffer. Consult with your family.
4 Identify the issues carefully and prioritise them. Analyse the grievance; identify who will suffer if the problem goes unchanged and how much suffering will occur. Be able to speak knowledgeably about the costs of inaction.
5 Know and be able to refer to the ethical standards of your professional association or trade union if you belong to one. Identify the laws and regulations which relate to the abuse. Identify organisational policies and documents which support correcting the abuse. Document everything thoroughly and double check your information.

Exhaust internal channels first

1 Take your complaint in writing, with appropriate supporting documents, to the authorities of your company or agency. Ask them to correct the abuse and give them fair warning that you may go outside if this is not done.
2 Exhaust all internal channels, making sure that your efforts to do so are well documented. This is by far the best method of choice for resolving the problem, *if* there are channels through which

you will be given a fair hearing. Give the organisation time to remedy the situation.

Protect yourself

1 Try to enlist others in the organisation to join you.
2 If possible, approach someone higher up in the organisation as a sounding board and to keep you informed of what is happening.
3 Stay on your best behaviour with superiors and peers. Work hard and do your job thoroughly. Bear in mind that all of your past performance may be reviewed if you blow the whistle; and that those you expose may retaliate or try to discredit you.
4 Know your legal rights and contact a good employment lawyer or someone who can advise you on your legal position. Know whether or not you are breaking any laws or terms of contracts, particularly those to do with confidentiality.
5 Look for another job.

Go outside only as a last resort

1 If all internal channels fail, you have several options: resign and speak out; stay and try to expose the abuse anonymously; stay and go public; stay and say nothing more. In any case, the benefits must be weighed against the likely risks.
2 You may choose to take your complaint to a statutory agency, like a regulatory body, or to expose it through the media, or go to a pressure group or a Member of Parliament. In any future legal action the courts will consider whether the recipient of the complaint was appropriate.
3 Be aware of the difficulties of blowing the whistle anonymously and, if you do, be prepared for your identity to be discovered. Remember that some third parties may not feel able to act on anonymous information.
4 Keep a log or diary of everything that happens, particularly at work, from the time you decide to take action.[12]

CONCLUSION

Employers who do not give employees with a concern a fair hearing create a time bomb for themselves and their employees and, possibly worse still, for the public. External whistleblowing can severely affect the future of the whistleblower and that of the organisation accused of malpractice. Ethical organisations legitimately require and must create improved channels for whistleblowing. To strike the right balance between confidentiality and business's responsibility to the wider community is now a pressing concern for all organisations. It is time that businesses realised that good business *is* ethical business.

Regulation from within is best achieved by making all employees personally responsible for the maintenance of the highest standards, and requiring them to report when those standards are breached, with no fear of reprisal. A workplace with clearly defined standards and clear procedures for reporting lapses will go a long way towards achieving this. When the internal systems of regulation fail, and even the most closely prescribed ones may do so at one time or another, the legal rights and duties of an employee who blows the whistle externally must be clear, as must the duties owed by the employee to the employer, and the role and efforts of professional associations, regulatory bodies, etc. in this area. At the moment, those hard working idealists who do blow the whistle are ill-supported and ultimately pay a heavy personal price for being the conscience of us all.

NOTES

1 British Institute of Management (1994) *Walking the Tightrope – A Survey of Ethics in Management*, Corby: BIM.
2 Winfield, Marlene (1990) *Minding your own Business: Self-regulation and Whistleblowing in British Companies*, London: Social Audit.
3 Soeken, Karen L. and Soeken, Donald R. (1987) *A Survey of Whistleblowers: Their Stressors and Coping Strategies*, Laurel, Md: Association of Mental Health Specialities.
4 Public Concern At Work (1994) *First Annual Report*, London: PCAW.
5 Glazer, M. P. and Glazer, P. M. (1986) 'The Whistleblower's Plight', *New York Times*, 13 August, p. A23.
6 For a detailed summary of the law as it relates to whistleblowers, see Rose, Nicholas (1995) 'Whistleblowing – Time for a Change', *NLJ Practitioner*, 27 January, pp. 113–15; see also IDS (1995) 'Whistleblowing', *IDS Brief No. 544*, July, pp. 7–12.
7 It should be noted that an August 1995 Court of Appeal judgement puts the future of this requirement in the balance. For a detailed discussion of this, see *IDS Brief No. 547*, August 1995, pp. 1–4.
8 Norton-Taylor, Richard (1995) 'Corporate Whistleblowers Set to Receive Protection they Deserve', *Guardian*, 6 December, p. 20.
9 Winfield, Marlene (1995) 'Whistleblowers as a Corporate Safety Net',

in Vinten, Gerald (ed.), *Whistleblowing: Subversion or Corporate Citizenship?*, London: Paul Chapman Publishing.

10 Ibid.

11 Winfield, Marlene, *Minding your own Business*, pp. 41–4. Winfield has also published a *summary* version of her whistleblowing book, under the same title. The whistleblower's checklist in this chapter is taken almost verbatim from this summary version, pp. 23–5.

12 For a manager's checklist that may help to deal effectively with a potential whistleblowing situation, see Ewing, David W. (1983) *Do it My Way or You're Fired*, New York: John Wiley, chapter 7.

Part III

SOME CURRENT TRENDS AND THEIR IMPACT ON BUSINESS ETHICS

INTRODUCTION TO PART III

Part III – *Some Current Trends and their Impact on Business Ethics*, has four contributions. So far, we have looked at some macro and micro issues in the field of business ethics in Parts I and II respectively. This final section identifies four major trends, all of which have implications for how we deal with the issues previously raised. It was necessary to be selective in choosing the four topics that follow, and the choice was made by asking, from a UK perspective, 'What are the relevant issues that are gathering momentum and which won't go away?' The outcome of pondering this question was: globalisation, gender, privatisation, and trade unions. This last one might seem to stand out from the others, but it is in the wider context of deregulation, and the shifting balance of power in favour of management, that its value lies. Indeed, power is a common underlying theme, the power of MNCs to act with few checks and balances, the changing power balance of men and women as reflected in the business world, the power of newly privatised industries in relation to their regulators, and the power of management in a climate of union de-recognition and lack of wages councils. As an ethical notion, therefore, exercising responsible power is a concern for all the contributors.

In Chapter 10, *Business Ethics and the Activities of Multinationals*, Bill Bain starts off with a vignette of President Clinton's ethical dilemma, in the light of his public commitment to uphold human rights, of whether to give China (post Tiananmen Square) the trade status of 'most-favoured-nation'. This sets the scene for exploring how Multinational Companies should conduct themselves when operating in host countries. The issues of cultural relativism and cultural imperialism are dealt with first, and, in rejecting both extremes, Bain goes on to examine three key questions concerning MNC activity. Drawing on the work of two leading writers in the field, he makes the case for MNCs being ethically bound to do no direct harm, to do more good than harm, and to uphold human rights while respecting local cultures. It was perhaps the Bhopal disaster of 1984 which emphasised for many the need for MNC regulation, but the issues are particularly complex and vexed. When developing 'host' countries deliberately lower safety standards in order to attract Western business, how should the latter respond? What supra-legal body can regulate MNCs which are everywhere and nowhere? How do we balance respect and tolerance for differing cultures, with our own national and organisational norms? Bain suggests some benchmarks of minimum standards which will help us to grapple effectively with such questions.

In Chapter 11, *Business Ethics and the Changing Gender Balance*, Heather Clark and Jim Barry make an incisive and comprehensive contribution in critically evaluating the (limited) research in this important and neglected area. If a 'caring 90s' ever emerges, to what extent will it have to do with more women entering the workforce? Will the increasing purchasing power of women force changes for the ethical better? Studies across cultures seem to suggest that women are more ethical than men; how true is this? Do women have to adopt male values in order to get to senior positions? Will companies started by women have a competitive advantage over 'male' companies? To what extent do men and women have different management styles? Such questions are examined in the context of emphasising gender *similarities*, as well as differences; there is unexplored significance in the fact that there are differences between men and differences between women, as well as between men and women. They conclude that, as a trend, gender has its significance properly in the context of gender 'as part of the wider social reality that is organisational life'. Teasing out pure gender differences from other influencing factors (such as class, ethnicity, age, religion, etc.) on behavioural differences will require further research, and the field is wide open.

In Chapter 12, *Privatised Ethics: The Case of the Regulated*

Utilities, Stephen Brigley and Peter Vass examine the rationality and fairness of public criticism of the privatised utilities, where the underlying public perception is that utilities (whether privatised or not) should conform to some 'higher' moral standard than everyday private businesses. The public criticism itself has usually focused on directors' pay, excessive profits and price increases, and inadequate public service, but the authors are concerned to get to the underlying ethical issues. They unearth first the ethical assumptions behind the advocates of 'private sector' and 'public service', by using stakeholder-rights to question those who uphold the notion that, for the utilities, a Friedmanite framework is ethically superior to a monopolistic one. The moral arguments surrounding differing regulatory frameworks are then examined in terms of the historical expectations of the public. Privatisation, they argue, has resulted in a fundamental shift in responsibility *from* government (despite the government's role in OFWAT, OFTEL, etc.) *to* individual companies and their directors. They argue that the old notion of 'public service' no longer suffices in such a changed environment, and that a stakeholder model, rather than a Friedmanite model, will better help utilities' directors fulfil their corporate responsibilities. Privatisation, perhaps more than anything else, has changed the face of Britain over the last seventeen years, and Brigley and Vass's chapter here makes a significant contribution in clarifying the debate.

Finally, in Chapter 13, *Trade Unions and Ethics: Unions as agents*, Patrick Flood and Philip Stiles make an interesting examination of another area hitherto neglected in the literature of business ethics – the implications of declining trade union membership and influence (something likely to continue with persistent high unemployment and the demise of traditional unionised industries). In particular, they focus on the dangers of a business environment where management is unconstrained by union presence. Can trade unions develop a new role for themselves as a regulatory ethical *and* economic mechanism, seen in a positive light by business? The authors make the case that, in both areas, the unions can, pointing out for example how new managerial techniques (such as HRM) have failed to replace trade unions, particularly in giving employees 'voice'. Additionally, individual bargaining often makes less economic and managerial sense than would a more collective approach; relying on individual entry/exit can be a very expensive way of defending a manager's right to manage. However, it seems that bringing this about will be difficult, due to both management's historical distrust of the unions, and the need for union leaders to perceive themselves in a new way.

The four areas which are addressed, globalisation, gender, privatisation and trade unions, are all (part of) key trends which will affect the extent to which notions of ethics will become embedded in business culture. Trying to predict how things will develop is probably less useful than attempting to recognise their significance in terms of contributing to some fundamental shifts in what is perceived as legitimate business activity. These four chapters also reflect generally increasing expectations for cultural sensitivity, equality of opportunity, distributive justice regarding our 'common inheritance', and for a genuine influence in company decision-making processes. They also map out the ethical bases of these expectations, and hence, in effect, call on business to defend its legitimacy and its 'licence to operate' by seriously taking such concerns on board – a task for both business managers and business ethics students alike.

10

BUSINESS ETHICS AND THE ACTIVITIES OF MULTINATIONALS

William A. Bain

INTRODUCTORY VIGNETTE

It was May of 1994, and US President Clinton was in the midst of an ethical conflict. No matter how he chose to act, he was sure to be accused of behaving unethically. In his 1992 election campaign he had attacked George Bush for extending trade privileges to China after its brutal crackdown in Tiananmen Square. China's human rights violations were condemned worldwide, and Clinton accused Bush of 'coddling criminals'.[1]

Clinton vowed that he was committed to human rights and, after coming to power, gave the Chinese government an ultimatum: improve your human rights record or your trade status as a 'most-favoured-nation' will not be renewed. Such a move would translate into a five- to ten-fold increase in American tariffs on Chinese goods, which would undoubtedly spark a trade war, further isolating China. Retaliatory measures against American multinationals operating in China would also be expected.

Instead of improving human rights, the Chinese government continued pretty much as usual. When it appeared that Clinton had no choice but to invoke tariffs, the year-long lobbying effort by American business hit its peak. At stake were sales to the world's single biggest market and fastest growing economy. China currently imports $8 billion of US goods annually – enough to keep 150,000 Americans employed – and these numbers are expected to increase drastically. Also at risk were opportunities for American businesses in China to continue to employ cheap labour. Letters and position papers were sent to the Clinton administration arguing that trade with China was critical to the American economy. In short, many felt that America could simply not afford to take the high moral ground.

This cry from America for 'business as usual' was a significant factor in Clinton's policy U-turn.[2] He severed the link between trade and human rights, and renewed China's trade status. Clinton justified this climbdown by saying that the cause of human rights would actually be advanced by ensuring that business continues with China. It was not a question of whether or not to keep pressing China's rulers on human rights but how best to do so. A key argument was that continued business with and in China would enhance working conditions, standards of living and economic freedom for Chinese workers. Some Chinese dissidents supported Clinton's decision and stated that it would bring democratic change in the long run. Other dissidents scoffed at this suggestion and claimed that America was supporting an oppressive regime.

INTRODUCTION AND PURPOSE

The above vignette sets the stage for a wide-ranging discussion on the ethical issues that arise in international business. For the purposes of this chapter, the emphasis will be on three themes:

1 The potential harm that can result when a multinational company (MNC) does business in a less developed country.
2 How one should act when faced with norms that differ from one's own.
3 What role individual companies and business associations should play in ensuring the ethical conduct of business.

The first theme was chosen because business has often behaved unethically and has caused suffering in less developed countries. The others were chosen because they are not particularly well understood by business practitioners. Each issue will be explored by turning first to some relevant points made by Richard T. De George in *Competing with Integrity in International Business*.[3] Before these themes can be reviewed, we must first discount two common positions which are seen by many as providing easy answers to ethical problems in international business.

CULTURAL RELATIVISM V. CULTURAL IMPERIALISM

One easy way to deal with ethical concerns that arise in international business is to deny that any special considerations are required. 'When in Rome, do as the Romans do.' If bribery is commonplace then it is acceptable to bribe. This doctrine, cultural relativism, is based on the reality that differences between cultures do exist. The belief is that it only makes sense to say that something is 'right' or 'wrong' in the context of a particular culture. If this were true, however, then an expatriate manager assigned to one of the pockets of the world where domestic servants are treated essentially as slaves, could herself have a slave.

Some values can only be evaluated relative to the context, but some moral norms are accepted by all. In no culture is it permissible to kill a neighbour arbitrarily (such actions could not be tolerated by any society, if only because it would surely mean that society would cease to function). There is widespread support for other basic norms, such as respecting human rights. What exactly is included as a human right needs to be debated. Even if one argues that the areas of agreement are small, cultural relativism 'offers no persuasive reason for seeing the international realm as a moral free-for-all in which anything goes'.[4]

At the opposite end of the spectrum is cultural imperialism. 'There is our way, and the wrong way.' This approach is based on the justifiable stance that one must not change one's ethics to suit the business environment. Some misinterpret this to mean that an MNC must operate in the same manner as it does at home and that MNC employees should try to assert their values on others. An expatriate manager would be correct to condemn a widespread local practice that discriminates against visible minorities. The fact that a practice is common does not make it acceptable. However, always operating with such a dogmatic approach is inappropriate, since many differences are not ethical in nature and there is no moral justification to challenge them.

If a family takes their car from England to Holland, they had better be prepared to drive on the right-hand side of the road. The norms pertaining to traffic regulations are not ethical in nature, even though we may talk about driving on 'the wrong side of the road'. However, not following the local traffic laws and thereby endangering others would be unethical. This is a case where the 'when in Rome' argument holds. There are business practices that, at first glance, appear to raise ethical conflicts, but under closer examination do not. As discussed later in this chapter, a foreigner may condemn what he sees as bribery but what really may be just a different way for officials to earn part of their salary.

The above two extreme views on approaching ethics in an international context have been discounted, while noting that each contains some truth. The difficulty in trying to determine how one should act when faced with norms which appear to conflict with one's own will be examined later.

POTENTIAL HARM BY MULTINATIONAL COMPANIES

The focus here is on the harm that can be done by MNCs in less developed countries (LDCs). This is of particular concern since these countries do not meet at the bargaining table as equals and are more susceptible to exploitation. As the outrage that resulted from the Bhopal disaster shows, we need to scrutinise more carefully the practices that MNCs adopt in LDCs.

Multinationals should respect the human rights of their employees[5]

This is an absolute minimum. Every individual has, for instance, the right to physical security and the right to subsistence regardless of a country's laws or norms. While the notion of respecting human rights is widely supported, there is debate as to what these fundamental rights are.[6] One agreement was reached in 1948 by the governments of the United Nations, as they adopted the Universal Declaration of Human Rights. This pledge has not been kept and it is the objective of organisations such as Amnesty International to press governments to observe it.[7]

Returning to the example of doing business in and with China, it is important to note that the use of forced labour has been documented. It would be an infringement of human rights to benefit from this labour. Appropriately, Clinton did uphold a ban on goods from forced labour camps. On the other hand, comments made by one top presidential aide call into question whether human rights really will be safeguarded by increased American–Chinese business. Commerce Secretary Ron Brown challenged the 'moral superiority' of those worrying about human rights in China more than economic growth in America.[8] Interestingly, human rights issues related to China's actions in Tibet appear to have played little part in the trade debate. China invaded Tibet in 1950 and claims it as an inalienable part of its territory. In the process of staking its claim, China perpetrated many atrocities, and human rights abuses are still being reported. The degree of American attention to these issues is increasing, in part due to a high profile 1995 tour of the USA made by the exiled Tibetan leader, the Dalai Lama.

Multinationals should do no intentional direct harm

This means, for example, that they should not dump hazardous waste or sell dangerous products. Such behaviour would be unethical even if it did not break host country laws. This guideline goes further than this (hopefully obvious) restriction by placing an extra duty on multinationals. If they feel that government officials have only their self-interest in mind, then it is up to the MNCs to consider the interests of all of those upon whom their actions may impact. If setting up an industrial complex in a Chinese agrarian province results in diverting or contaminating a major water source, the company cannot claim that it is in no way responsible for any starvation that may result, even if some Chinese government officials actively supported the project.

MNCs prefer to operate in stable countries, and have been accused of supporting oppressive regimes in order to maintain stability. Some Chinese political dissidents believe that America is aiding such a regime by not linking trade with human rights. It is doubtful that American business leaders would want oppression in order to have cheap labour. At the same time, they had a duty during their lobbying efforts to examine the issue of human rights and not just conveniently ignore it.

Multinationals should produce more good than harm for the host country

This guideline prevents MNCs from justifying their actions on a miscalculation of utility gained. It may be that a particular operation would ultimately harm a small number of people in an LDC but provide benefits for a far greater number of foreign consumers. Some strip mining and mass deforestation activities arguably fall into this category. Such activities cannot be justified on a utilitarian ground since, in the long run, they widen the gulf between the First and Third Worlds, and thereby increase global tensions.

A key point made by the American business lobby during the Chinese trade debate was that American business serves as a positive force for change. Conditions and economic freedom for Chinese workers are said to be improving. The American policy supposedly 'encourages Chinese cooperation in building a new regional and international order based upon peace and security'.[9] Indeed, some Chinese dissidents agree that American business is a vehicle for beneficial change.

In many ways the case for doing business in China parallels the debate about business's involvement in apartheid South Africa. With reference to this particular guideline, it is often difficult to determine if more good than harm is being generated. Some businesses pulled out of South Africa because they feared that they were supporting an immoral regime, while others stayed and argued that their presence would help bring about change. Now that apartheid has been dismantled, both sides are claiming victory.

DOING BUSINESS IN A CULTURE WITH DIFFERENT NORMS

As suggested in the discussion on ethical relativism and imperialism, it is very hard to determine how one should behave when confronted with norms that are very much different from one's own. This issue will be examined by first turning to one of De George's guidelines: 'To the extent that local culture does not violate ethical norms, multinationals should respect the local culture and work with and not against it.'

The justification for this guideline can be simply stated – it must be followed in order to prevent the MNC from harming the host. Translating this norm into specific action plans, however, may be one of the biggest ethical challenges that an MNC employee faces. One must determine both how an MNC's activities might negatively impact upon the host's culture, and how any adverse effects can be minimised. A key to the solution is to make a concerted effort to understand the host culture.

Culture can be defined as the way a group of people solves its problems. For a variety of reasons (historical, geographic, climatic, etc.) cultures have created specific solutions for certain problems. Some place a high value on individual achievement while others emphasise the need for a strong collective. In some it is acceptable to express emotion, while in others, objectivity and detachment are preferred.[10]

Cultural differences will produce actions that may or may not raise ethical concerns. An expatriate may be taken aback when he witnesses the host culture's decision-making process, but it might not be wrong – only different. If so, then it is an ethical requirement to honour it. (It also is arguably just plain good business sense to do so.) Understanding the culture will help determine if there is an ethical problem. But empathy does not lead to relativism.

Say a culture's emphasis on the collective manifests itself in practices that maintain a traditional view of the extended family. Nepotism occasionally occurs, and women are discouraged from working. If one believes that such actions violate individuals' rights (and some may argue that this depends on one's definition of human rights), the MNC should not follow these local norms. Widespread unethical behaviour is not justification for following suit. De George stops short of saying that an MNC should take an active role outside its own walls to try to change the offending custom.

Donaldson addresses this issue differently, through an ethical algorithm. According to him, the first step in addressing a clash between home and host country norms is to determine whether the moral reasons underlying the host country's view relate to its relative level of economic development. This approach is required because it is easiest for us to empathise with the almost universally shared desire for economic wellbeing. If the disagreement is not a function of economic development, then our inability to empathise forces us to take a minimalist view. It is morally acceptable for someone to undertake a practice that is not the norm at home but is so in the host country, if it is a requirement of doing business and human rights are not violated.[11]

Here we return to the necessity of understanding the host culture. While Donaldson makes the point that it is hard to empathise, we must make an effort to do so, even if it is only to apply his algorithm correctly. Donaldson analyses the practice of low-level 'bribery' of customs officials in some South American countries.[12] Fees are small, uniformly assessed and (presumably) openly collected. This is identified as a conflict independent of economic development and is acceptable according to the algorithm. Payments are not a direct violation of a fundamental international right, and are required to conduct business successfully. The conclusion of a foreigner forced to deal with the customs official may then be that the country is corrupt, at least at this level.

However, it cannot be assumed, without first understanding the culture, that this case is independent of economic development. Indeed, many cash-strapped LDCs pay their officials very little and allow them to supplement their wages. This is analogous to the culturally accepted practice in many countries of mandatory surcharges in restaurants being passed on to the staff. If this is the correct interpretation, then the conclusion of a foreigner using the algorithm would likely be that the practice, incorrectly referred to as 'bribery', is acceptable – not unethical but tolerable.

Another key reason for understanding the culture is to ensure that the practices being questioned by the visiting MNC really reflect the beliefs of the people (i.e. the culture) and are not just the self-interested wishes of the ruling elite.

Returning to the example of doing business in China, an American spokesman for a business coalition said: 'Our Chinese employees, managers, and workers are exposed to Western values, encouraged to think independently, and offered opportunities previously unavailable in China'.[13] It cannot be assumed that all of this will be beneficial for the Chinese, as this American is claiming to be the case. Some Western values would no doubt upset the local culture. By turning to a cultural model such as the one referenced above, visitors are better able to identify how their activities may harm their host, and what can be done to minimise the impact.

THE ROLE BUSINESS SHOULD PLAY IN ENSURING ETHICAL BUSINESS

The final theme of this chapter is what role, if any, individual companies and business associations should play in ensuring the ethical conduct of business. According to De George, 'Multinationals should cooperate with the local government in developing and enforcing just background institutions.'

MNCs should support local government initiatives such as those aimed at protecting human rights, fair competition and the environment. Some contend that this would not be in a company's self-interest, and is therefore not a realistic expectation. For a company that is committed to behaving ethically, and it does take commitment, this is a flawed, short-term view. If an LDC is able to develop these characteristics, then business would occur on an even playing field. Companies would compete on merit, and the opportunity for any immediate gains that unethical players had in the past (e.g. by bribing officials or exploiting workers) would not be tolerated.

In parallel to cooperating with such endeavours, companies can form self-regulating associations. One example of this is the chemical industry's Responsible Care Programme. The manufacturers publicly acknowledge what their responsibilities are with respect to the safe manufacturing, transportation, use and disposal of their products. The code is powerful because it recognises that the public ultimately grants the firms' licences to operate. Self-regulation is arguably more powerful than international law.

Turning back once again to the case of business in China, it is disturbing to note the reaction to a proposal from Clinton that a voluntary code of conduct be created for American business in China to address human rights. The president of the American Chamber of Commerce in Beijing said that business was willing to discuss this, but most American executives have said that their companies follow their own business ethics codes.[14] An unwillingness to follow up on Clinton's suggestion leaves one with the fear that the *status quo* falls short of the above guideline. Each company might look after its own short-term interest and not cooperate with other initiatives.

There is a parallel here between the rationale used on the level of the firm and that on the national and international level. For many ethical issues, progress can be made only by seeking a solution on the next level. The Responsible Care Programme became most effective when an American association adopted what was a Canadian initiative and 'exported' it to many other nations.

One argument that carried weight during the trade debate was that, if America does not do business with China, other countries will fill the void. Historical evidence suggests this is correct. (When US President Jimmy Carter tried to stop grain shipments to the Soviet Union, Canada and Australia benefited by making up some of the shortfall.[15]) As a spokesman for the Chinese Foreign Minister pointed out, China has trade relationships with over 200 countries and regions and 'does not have this problem with any of the rest of them'.[16] By acting unilaterally in this dispute with China, America stood to lose in two ways: the policy objectives would not be met, and markets would be lost to Americans. As with many other initiatives, if trade sanctions truly are to work, they must be addressed on an international level.

SUMMARY

The sphere of international business presents many unique challenges for the multinational company committed to ethical business. As the case with American companies doing business in and with China illustrates, there are no easy answers.

⌐In order for MNCs to behave ethically, employees must be aware of the potential for harm. They must respect human rights, do no intentional direct harm and do more good than harm.

Employees of multinationals are often confronted with norms that differ from their own. A thorough understanding of the host country's culture is required to determine if the conflict is ethical in nature. One must try to respect the local culture but not go so far as to violate universal ethical norms.

Individual companies and business associations have a special role to play in ensuring the ethical conduct of business. Not only should they cooperate with their hosts in establishing background institutions, they should create self-regulating bodies to address their own concerns. To be effective in doing so, they may need to elevate the discussion to the next level.⌐

NOTES

1 *The Washington Post*, 27 May 1994, p. A28.
2 Other factors included a desire to recruit China's assistance in pressuring North Korea to abandon its nuclear weapons programme, and an attempt to have more influence over China in order to get it to sign a global nuclear test ban treaty. *The Washington Post*, 27 May 1994, p. A28.
3 Published by Oxford University Press, New York, 1993. No brief summary of this work can do justice to the material covered and, as a result, De George's book should be considered a 'must read' by those who want to study this topic in depth. (NB: see *Further Reading*, p. 193).
4 Donaldson, Thomas (1989) *The Ethics of International Business*, New York: Oxford University Press; p. 19. (NB: this book is also a key reference for those studying this topic. See *Further Reading*, p. 193).
5 The guidelines discussed here are from De George, *Competing with Integrity in International Business*, chapter 3.
6 Donaldson addresses rights and provides guidance on what conditions must be satisfied when they are defined. See Donaldson, *The Ethics of International Business*, chapter 5.
7 For a description of Amnesty International's activities and objectives, along with a reprint of the UN's Universal Declaration of Human

Rights, see Staunton, Marie and Fenn, Sally (eds) (1990) *The Amnesty International Handbook*, London: Macdonald Optima.

8 *The Wall Street Journal*, 31 May 1994, p. A18.

9 American Secretary of State Warren Christopher, *The New York Times*, 28 May 1994, p. 5.

10 See Trompenaars, Fons (1993) *Riding the Waves of Culture*, London: Nicholas Brealey Publishing. Trompenaars has created a model to explain cultural diversity in business. A culture's solution to universal problems can described by seven fundamental dimensions which fit into three different categories: relationships with people (universalism v. particularism, individualism v. collectivism, neutral v. emotional, specific v. diffuse, achievement v. ascription); attitudes to time; and attitudes to the environment.

11 Donaldson, *The Ethics of International Business*, pp. 101–6. His basic argument is this: if a practice is not morally and/or legally permitted in the home country but is so in the host country, then the conflict is one of two types. If the moral reasons underlying the host country's view that the practice is permissible refer to the host country's relative level of economic development, one can conclude that the practice is not permissible if: *The members of the home country would not, under conditions of economic development relevantly similar to those of the host country, regard the practice as permissible.*

   If the moral reasons underlying the host country's view are independent of the level of economic development, the practice is determined to be not permissible if either of the following criteria are true:

   1 It is possible to conduct business successfully in the host country without undertaking the practice.
   2 The practice is a direct violation of a fundamental international right.

12 Donaldson, *The Ethics of International Business*, p. 104.

13 *The New York Times*, 28 May 1994, p. 5.

14 *The Washington Post*, 28 May 1994, p. A24.

15 Ibid., p. A28.

16 Ibid.

11

BUSINESS ETHICS AND THE CHANGING GENDER BALANCE

Heather Clark and Jim Barry

INTRODUCTION

Increasing attention is being paid to the study of business ethics at a time when more and more women are entering the workforce in Western industrialised societies. As it is commonly believed in the literature on gender and business ethics that women tend to be more ethical than men, we explore the implications for business activity. We focus here on the role of gender and ethics in the management and organisation of work on which a number of recent studies have reported. In time we hope that research effort will enhance and extend our understanding of these and other issues including, for example, the impact that increased female spending power might have on advertising, consumer products[1] and ethical investments. For now we focus on the management and control of work. In this chapter we outline the context in which research on gender and business ethics has developed, consider some of the major findings on the role of gender and ethics in the management and organisation of work, and discuss the issues raised.

THE CONTEXT FOR THE DEVELOPMENT OF INTEREST IN GENDER AND BUSINESS ETHICS

Gender and business ethics is a relatively under-researched area of enquiry which has been receiving increasing attention in recent years. The reasons for this are probably quite complex. Ideas always seem to have their time. Certainly in the field of business and management studies, fashions and fads are not unknown, leading Drucker[2] to conclude that business ethics generally was becoming the 'in' subject and might well be termed 'ethical chic'. Interest in business ethics is not new historically, of course,[3] though recent concerns about scandal,[4] moral decline,[5] deregulation,[6] and global interdependence[7] has raised its profile. Awareness of cross cultural differences in business ethics have undoubtedly fuelled debate between what have been called 'ethical imperialists', those wishing to spread their own ethnocentric view of right and wrong, and 'moral relativists', who seem paralysed when confronted with equally objective and seemingly incompatible 'truths' – who are we, they argue, to decry or gainsay a bribe when it is seen as normal and is commonplace business practice in a foreign country.

Mayer and Cava[8] wrestle with just such dilemmas in their account of gender equality for American multinational companies, who are required to follow Title V11 of the Civil Rights Act of 1964, which prohibits discrimination in employment, in their overseas operations. They show how, for example, in Saudi Arabia laws exist which prevent women from 'travelling alone, working with men' and 'working with non-Muslim foreigners'; these laws, they remind us, apply equally to foreigners as well as to indigenous women in the host society. Japan, on the other hand, has laws which, in theory at least, promote gender equality – though traditional patriarchal practices, which serve to keep women in a subordinate position in the workplace and home, remain to confound them. *Their* advice is to muddle on in good faith so that, in time, the exchange of values and enhanced understanding of difference will lead to greater tolerance all round.

Yet awareness of cross-cultural interdependence and the heightened profile of ethics in business seem unlikely reasons alone to account for the recent interest in gender and business ethics. It may not be a coincidence that a country in which research into gender and business ethics is gaining ground was also one of the first to experience the rise of what has been called a 'women's movement', a social and political movement for change, sometimes referred to as 'second-wave feminism'. This term serves both to distinguish current from earlier concerns about gender inequality and also to keep alive an awareness of the historical continuities in women's disadvantaged position in society generally. The issue of gender inequality was raised in the 1960s, the 'decade of protest', when a number of other movements, including those for Civil Rights and Peace, made their voices heard – quite independently of the later interest in business ethics.

Just as there is no one thing called 'business ethics', however, neither is there one women's movement, one feminism or feminist position. Indeed, as the 1960s turned into the 1970s, a number of different perspectives on women in Western societies became clear, in particular: Liberal Feminism, whose advocates largely supported the *status quo* and argued for legal change through policies of equal opportunity; Socialist and Marxist Feminism, which focused on individual freedoms and whose supporters sought change in the features of bourgeois capitalist societies and remedies through workplace struggle; and Radical and Revolutionary Feminism, whose adherents went to the root of the problem in patriarchal societies and labelled men as the problem and the main enemy. Liberal and Radical Feminism have tended to dominate the American scene, with the Socialist and Marxist varieties more commonly found in Europe.

With heightened awareness of gender inequality, a number of developments took place from the 1980s onwards. On a practical level, women began the attempt to enter the circles of elite male privilege in greater numbers – with the backing of legislation on equal opportunity and sexual discrimination. In ever-increasing numbers, women began slowly to attain senior positions in established institutions.[9] These included local and central government, the corporate world and the established professions, at a time of worldwide economic and political turbulence.

On a theoretical level, a number of interesting research projects and texts were undertaken, leading to a number of significant developments in our understanding of gender and the role of women and men in organisational life. The latest of these draws attention to the differences *between* women, highlighted initially by so-called 'Black Feminism',[10] and questions the usefulness and meaning of the very categories of gender themselves (the terms 'woman' and 'man'), a position associated with a school of thought known as post-structuralism and identified with the work of the French philosopher Foucault.[11] Not all of these ideas have filtered through to the literature on gender and business ethics, which has tended to reflect Liberal and Radical influences and is concerned more with individualism, equality of opportunity and differences between women and men, though they are of considerable importance for future research efforts and will be returned to later in this chapter.

THE LITERATURE ON GENDER AND BUSINESS ETHICS

Studies in the literature invariably point to a number of factors which have stimulated research into gender and business ethics. These are identified as follows: first, there are more women entering the workforce, and equal opportunity policies are increasingly to be found in Western industrialised countries; second, more women are enrolling on courses in business schools, promising a significant rise in female executives in years ahead; and third, women are making inroads generally into management and corporate governance.[12] Finally, and perhaps most important of all, it is believed that women are in general terms more ethically inclined than men, and there is interest in the implications of this for business activity.[13] Barnett and Karson[14] helpfully summarise what are held to be the domain or background assumptions of the literature, namely that:

> women are: (1) more concerned about relationships than men; (2) define themselves through relationships, as opposed to men, and, most importantly; (3) select actions in terms of supporting relationships and/or being approved by others, as opposed to men, who follow absolute rules and principles that are separate from relationships.

Barnett and Karson argue that these differences derive somehow from the 'different socialization pressures on boys and girls'. They may, however, overstate the argument,[15] since there is some measure of confusion, if not disagreement, in the literature over whether women and men do in fact have different ethical values, exhibit different ethical behaviour, and take differently those decisions which could be construed as containing one or more ethical components. To add to the confusion, Burke *et al.*[16] suggest that women in senior business and professional positions, in British business at least, may have a less ethical stance on business matters compared to other issues such as the environment. We consider here a few examples of recent research to make the point. First we look at those who see no real difference between women and men, and then at those who do.

Sikula and Costa[17] surveyed 211 students from a California State University Management and Organisation course and repeated their questionnaires some ten weeks later to double-check their results. They indicate that 171 'usable pairs' of questionnaires were produced. Using the four ethical values of Equality, Freedom, Honesty and Responsibility, they report *no* significant differences between women and men. Their major finding: that female business students were not more ethical than male. They conclude their paper, however, by noting that there *were* significant differences between women and men in their ranking of the following dimensions (which were used to construct their four major ethical values):

- 'A World at Peace' and 'Forgiving', which women valued more than men; and
- 'An Exciting Life' and 'Imaginative', which men valued more than women

They refer to these as 'non-ethical values', a curious conclusion for the categories 'A World at Peace' and 'Forgiving', which seem closely related to the ethical concern about relationships identified by Barnett and Karson as we saw earlier. Sikula and Costa's conclusion, that women and men exhibit no significant ethical differences, is therefore somewhat difficult to sustain and may have resulted from the research methodology they employed. The point here is that the matter is not entirely clear.

We find some uncertainty also in the research work of Barnett and Karson themselves,[18] who focus on American executives. They see *some* differences in gender terms, but are struck by complicating factors which cloud the picture considerably. They note, for example, some age and career-stage differences, reporting that 'later "career stage" groups in total are more ethical than early groups.' So, too, in the work of Crow *et al.*,[19] whose female student respondents were seen to be at a 'higher stage' of moral development than the respective males. While this might *seem* important, however, they urge caution in interpretation since their women respondents might be atypical; they advocate further research. Both these studies were conducted on relatively small samples.

A good example of a study which argued that there *were* important ethical differences between women and men, which is worth considering here, is that by Harris,[20] particularly as efforts were made to replicate aspects of his research some years later by Galbraith and Stephenson.[21] Harris argued that, in general terms, research showed that business students had lower ethical values than other students. In recent years, however, women, who were thought to be more ethically inclined than men, were being attracted to business courses in ever-greater numbers. Harris set out to explore the issues, conducting research on 161 American 'graduating seniors'. Somewhat contrary to expectation, he found little difference in the ethical values held by female and male students, though he did note that, for the most part, women students were 'significantly less tolerant of questionable business practice', and that there were some important differences in *how* women and men made decisions (the *process*) The women, he argued, used an approach which favoured that which was good for the majority (utilitarian) rather than maximising self interest (egoist) – even if they eventually arrived at the same decision.

This issue of the decision process was taken up specifically by Galbraith and Stephenson[22] who also surveyed 'graduating seniors' in an American business school – in all a total of 107 students were involved. They found some support for Harris's thesis – that women tended to be utilitarian whereas men were egoist – though the results were not dramatic in this respect. They do note, however, that while there was little difference in the use of decision criteria generally between women and men, there might well be more differences within each group. That is, there may be more discernible differences *between women* and *between men*, than differences *between women and men* (it is worth noting here Goffee's[23] acknowledgment of differences between European women managers in terms of 'age . . . occupation, organisational context and national culture') Galbraith and Stephenson further argue that, despite this, women are more likely to 'invoke different decision rules for different ethical situations, while men seem to exhibit less diversity in their use of ethical decision rules'.[24] The use of the word 'diversity' is interesting here, with its connotations of deviance and diversion – consider the impact on the meaning of this conclusion if the word 'flexibility' had been used instead, with its overtones of versatility. These are important issues to which we return later.

The final study we consider here is that by Ruegger and King,[25] who also used American student respondents, though with a sample size higher than those reviewed so far (they used completed questionnaires from 2196 students, of whom 111 were classified as 'international' students). They also conducted follow-up 'voluntary class discussions'. They consider gender *and* age, and argue that both are significant in determining ethical conduct and the perception of ethical business situations. Their findings can be summarised as follows:

Women are more ethical than men with respect to:

1 performing work or engaging in practices that may be unethical or harmful;
2 employer's responsibility for the safety and welfare of its workers;
3 informing on your employer; and
4 the company's duty to restrain itself when there is a lack of competition.

There are no significant differences between women and men in respect of:

5 using company time for personal business; and
6 informing on fellow employees.

In only one case, 'informing on fellow employees', was there no significant age difference. On all other dimensions, the older the respondent the more ethical the response. The most ethical age group, accordingly, was 40-plus, followed by the others in turn: 31–40, 22–30 and those below 22 years of age.

Once more the importance of socialisation is acknowledged as playing a role. Their speculation on this, however, is restricted to a few comments on the family where, it is held, men are taught to be 'aggressive' and women to be 'loving and caring'.

DISCUSSION

We wish to highlight three areas for discussion: first, the issue of sampling and the representativeness of the literature; second, the changing place of women in the workforce; and third, the belief that there are likely to be differences between women and men which would be of interest in the study of gender and business ethics. We will make a few comments about the first two areas and focus most of the discussion on the third. Our purpose is to draw out the underlying assumptions of the literature on gender and business ethics for examination and critical discussion. Our consideration of issues is not exhaustive, and we would encourage others to engage critically with the literature in order to identify further assumptions. Our view is that *assumptions* exist to be explored in a spirit of free critical enquiry.

Representative samples?

A great deal of the literature preoccupies itself with small samples of business students and occasionally some executives; they are often American and are invariably asked to complete question-naires. There is nothing 'wrong' or otherwise 'questionable' about this *per se* but it does raise important questions about generalisa-tion.

This is a point understood and normally acknowledged in the lit-erature. Of the studies considered here, for example, we can report that Barnett and Karson[26] were concerned that theirs was 'not a random sample', claiming their work to be 'exploratory'. Likewise Harris[27] cautions the reader against generalisation, while Crow *et al.*[28] argue that workplace studies are much needed. Sikula and Costa[29] also accept the limited character of their sample of business students, acknowledging:

> the always present research limitation of whether paper and pencil manipulations can appropriately forecast real, actual behaviour. Just because some students rank certain values ahead of others does not prove that their actual behaviors will be more or less ethical than other people activities.

The widespread use of questionnaire surveys is also a point worth considering. Sets of predetermined questions always run the risk of misinterpretation by the respondent, even if fully piloted; and there remains a further problem of interpretation for the researcher when viewing the results. Further, answers will be dir-ected to the questions asked, which may be subtly biased in ways unseen by the researcher; and it is never known how far the answers of the non-respondents would have affected the results. No one research method is perfect, however, and all have their limitations. What is needed is a circumspect or wary eye on the part of the researcher and some degree of humility in the presentation of results and claims for generalisability. The wider use of in-depth interviewing might also be encouraged, in an effort to get beyond the current preoccupation with measurable forms of quantitative data in order to gain access to the rich world of qualitative material inaccessible to the resolute 'number-cruncher'.

A final point worth noting is the predominance of American cases in the growing literature, although there has been interest shown in business ethics from a European perspective, evidenced by the emergence in 1992 of the journal *Business Ethics: A European Review*. As we saw when considering the context in which the study of business ethics developed, there is an inclination to focus on individual and equal opportunity with its roots in the prevailing political orthodoxy of Liberalism, and on differences between women and men. This is as true of the European as the American literature at present, and may limit generalisation, a point we return to later in the chapter.

The changing place of women in the workforce

We noted earlier in this chapter that the literature under consideration assumes the existence of a growing number of women entering the workforce, and that there are more women enrolling on business courses and making inroads into managerial elites in a context of increasingly equal opportunities. To some degree, of course, this is an accurate depiction of reality, though it is worth sounding, in particular, two notes of caution.

First, statistics on changes in the labour force in Western countries *do* show a tendency for increasing numbers of women to take jobs. But the positions they are attaining are often part-time and insecure. In Britain the Equal Opportunities Commission (EOC) reports regularly on relative differences between women and men. The factsheet 'Some Facts About Women' is produced annually, and is available from the EOC on request (details are given at the end of the chapter). Drawing on official sources such as the *Labour Force Survey* and the Department of Employment, the factsheets make for interesting reading, as they document clear and continuing disparities in position and representation between women and men. Women, for example, have consistently earned less than men (figures in the 1994 factsheet are given for 1975, when female earnings were 71 per cent of male, and 1993 when they were 79 per cent, for full-time employees, excluding overtime; see also de Bruijn[30]), and are heavily concentrated in part-time rather than full-time paid employment.[31]

Second, for those women who enter senior or managerial positions, breaking through what has been called the 'Glass Ceiling',[32] we find further evidence to suggest that, far from having somehow 'made it', they continue to suffer discrimination and disadvantage. The reasons are many and include a male network,[33] male resistance to gender equality[34] and the male 'backlash',[35] as well as heightened pressures on middle and senior managers. This is notable in particular for women in the public sector in the UK, as it undergoes rapid and significant restructuring and change.[36] There is also research which suggests that women suffer more stress at work than men.[37] Little wonder that the number of women managers, after increasing for some time, has plateaued.[38]

Differences between women and men?

There is, of course, an ethical question involved in undertaking research which looks for differences between women and men – whether the research concerns ethics or not. Quite apart from the more usual questions of confidentiality, what if we find differences we do not like or approve of?

Scarr[39] argues that academics should ask questions about both 'racial and gender differences', even if the results do not prove popular. This is a controversial argument which has exercised the likes of Jensen and Eysenck in studies of Intelligence Quotient (IQ) as applied to race. Equally, the argument which goes 'well, I may have designed the bomb, but I'm not responsible for how it's used' cannot be pushed too far, though what the debates *have* highlighted is a requirement for responsibility in research. In Scarr's case she contends that there is also a need to be careful not to assume the values of the host group in how the questions are asked and findings interpreted; i.e. we should not assume that any differences found are automatically to be viewed negatively or as deviant – they may equally well be viewed positively, a point we return to presently.

The idea of difference, of a 'female ethic', according to Grimshaw,[40] can be traced directly to the eighteenth-century context of industrialising societies, where the idealised vision of womanly virtue expressed through family life reigned supreme – an idea viewed with suspicion, it must be said, by a number of women who noticed that 'virtue' had become associated with a role that was simultaneously subordinate. The notion that women are more virtuous than men, and that this should be valued and celebrated, nonetheless survives today – at least among some women. The importance of women's role in the Peace Movement, for example, might *just* be interpreted in this light if women are seen as caring and nurturant, and less likely to press a nuclear button than men, though this line of argument need not rely on a belief that such differences are in some way 'natural' or 'God-given' – difference can be accounted for as a *social* phenomenon. The real issue is the way in which difference, if it exists in any sense, is interpreted – negatively or positively. This point is precisely the one developed by Gilligan in her book *In A Different Voice: Psychological Theory and Women's Development*.[41] Tribute to her work is paid by some researchers into gender and business ethics; of those discussed here, for example, Barnett and Karson and Crow *et al.*[42] acknowledge their intellectual debt.

Gilligan's starting point is a reaction to theories of moral development in children associated with the likes of Kohlberg and Piaget. In essence they conceptualised moral development as growth through a series of stages which lead to higher levels of reasoning based on rules, principles and abstract logic, a model which appeared to be congruent with the development of boys. Girls were seen as wanting from this viewpoint, judged, as they were, according to norms 'set' by the boys. Gilligan examines their arguments and accepts a number of points, but disputes their interpretation. Boys do develop in this way, she concedes, whereas for girls:

> the outline of a moral conception different from that described by Freud, Piaget or Kohlberg begins to emerge and informs a different description of development. In this conception, the moral problem arises from conflicting responsibilities rather than from competing rights and requires for its resolution a mode of thinking that is contextual and narrative rather than formal and abstract. This conception of morality as concerned with the activity of care centers moral development around the understanding of responsibility and relationships, just as the conception of morality as fairness ties moral development to the understanding of rights and rules.[43]

Gilligan uses a number of case studies involving in-depth interviewing to construct her arguments, and uses excerpts from them to illustrate her points. Her interviews with two eleven-year-olds, Jake and Amy, are illuminating and worth recounting here. Jake and Amy were asked to resolve an ethical dilemma, devised by Kohlberg and known as the 'Heinz dilemma'. Gilligan explains:

> In this particular dilemma, a man named Heinz considers whether or not to steal a drug which he cannot afford to buy in order to save the life of his wife. In the standard format of Kohlberg's interviewing procedure, the description of the

144

dilemma itself – Heinz's predicament, the wife's disease, the druggist's refusal to lower his price – is followed by the question, 'Should Heinz steal the drug?'[44]

Jake argues that Heinz *should* steal the drug. He weighs various arguments, which concern rights and priorities concerning such matters as the value of human life, and applies rules and logic. He suggests that, if Heinz is caught, then the Judge would probably reason in much the same way and be lenient. Amy, on the other hand, considers whether Heinz should *steal* the drug (note the difference in emphasis here). She wonders if the money could be borrowed or the druggist informed of the dilemma. Once everyone becomes aware of the problem, Amy feels a solution will be found. Rather than ignoring the problem, waffling, or missing the point (all negative interpretations of her reasoning), she sees a complex narrative of relationships and a human problem amenable to resolution by caring people – not a hypothetical problem to be resolved abstractly. Gilligan argues that this results from early psychological development whereby girls develop an 'ethic of care' and boys learn a 'logic of justice'.

In a telling comment, Gilligan suggests that women are more inclined to change rules in order to preserve relationships whereas men are more likely to abide by rules, seeing relationships as replaceable. Women thus draw on their direct experience of life with other people in order to explore *real life* dilemmas or 'concrete' situations – a point which might help to explain Galbraith and Stephenson's[45] finding noted earlier in the chapter (see p. 139) that women displayed greater 'diversity' than men in the case of ethical decision rules. Interesting though it is, there are problems with Gilligan's work: it rests, for example, on a limited number of case studies and it accepts gender difference – an argument seen by some as ammunition for those who would seize on it as proof that a woman's place is in the home and reverse the precious few advances that *have* been made for women in society. If, however, we do acknowledge difference, but view it positively, she argues, we may have a way forward which recognises difference of other kinds – difference due, for example, to social class and ethnicity – to help us to achieve a fuller understanding of the complexities of social life.

This argument is extended by Benhabib,[46] who locates developmental theories of the Kohlberg type within a specific patriarchal and bourgeois context. The dominant ideology in this context is

Liberal political theory, which shares with moral development theory a belief in abstract philosophy – to which we might also add equality of opportunity and individualism. Associated with followers of the English philosopher Hobbes and the French encyclopedist Rousseau, these theorists conceptualised citizens as 'generalised others', as autonomous individuals invested with rights and obligations who, in a 'state of nature', as 'noble savages', would come to agree on the very basis of social order and the rules and procedures to be put in place to regulate its harmonious functioning. Here again, Benhabib argues, there is a preoccupation with disembodied abstractions:

> a strange world; it is one in which individuals are growing up before they have been born; in which boys are men before they have been children; a world where neither mother, nor sister nor wife exist . . . are these individuals *human selves* at all?[47]

Her argument against this dominant mode of thinking is that individuals are human beings, whose identities come to be forged through experience and who have different individual life histories which are formed in different ways, not just in terms of gender but also in respect of race, class, culture, psychic and natural abilities.

So who are these 'real' people, these 'concrete others' that Benhabib refers to; what has been their experience? What evidence is there that considers the role of 'real' women in existing senior managerial positions? Three studies throw light on this for our purposes, three studies which acknowledge difference, but *also* point to the enduring nature of social structural factors which weigh heavily on the shoulders of women *as* women – those by Ferguson, Rosener and Lunneborg.[48] These studies use American examples, the context for much of the research on gender and business ethics, though their analyses stretch the boundaries of the dominant ideology of Liberalism; not concerned specifically with ethics, their work nonetheless provides valuable insights.

Burke *et al.*[49] argue that women in senior business and professional positions in Britain tend to be less ethical when it comes to business matters than they are over issues related, for example, to the environment. The work of Ferguson,[50] which draws on the work of Gilligan and to some extent Foucault's post-structuralist theory, may help us to understand why. Ferguson argues that the experiences of women do not equip them particularly well to fit into existing bureaucratic organisations, whose structures and cultures reflect a logic of justice associated with male values. While women continue to accept these prevailing values and conform in order to gain access to organisations and secure promotion within them, in line with Liberal orthodoxy, organisational relations will continue to reflect male priorities (see also Acker[51]). That this may be the existing reality, at least in Britain, is suggested by Burke et al.'s research. Their comments are worth quoting:

> It is . . . possible that women that are successful in business . . . are successful because of their tough business attitude. It could be that one can only succeed in business, regardless of sex, by being hard nosed over ethical niceties.[52]

Rosener,[53] however, reports details of a survey 'sponsored by the International Women's Forum' and argues that women managers in medium-sized, non-traditional organisations are using their experiences to create a leadership style which she calls 'interactive leadership', in which they 'encourage participation, share power and information, enhance other people's self-worth, and get others excited about their work'. Women thus lead differently to men. The survey consisted of women in organisations which were experiencing turbulence and rapid change and provided opportunities for the women that may not be available in other settings. The findings may thus be atypical, though they do mirror to some degree the extensive research undertaken by Lunneborg.

Lunneborg[54] conducted a number of interviews with women in senior positions within what she describes as male-dominated occupations: physician, lawyer, manager, landscape architect, stockbroker, state legislator, firefighter, police officer, electrician and carpenter. She found important differences in the way women worked. They had:

- A service orientation to clients
- A nurturant approach to co-workers
- An insistence upon a balanced life-style
- An attraction to managing others using power differently than men did[55]

Generally the women had entered these occupations out of *choice* and viewed their jobs and their careers positively. They were not working just for the money but were interested in their work and wanted to enjoy their (working) lives as far as they were able; they were thus less vulnerable to bribery. According to

Lunneborg, this positive evaluation led women to positive views of their roles, far removed from the externally imposed stereotypical roles reported by Kanter[56] of 'Iron Maiden', 'Pet' and 'Seductress'. They may well have brought 'sex-role stereotyped attributes and actions' to their workplaces, but they did so as competitive, ambitious and hard-working women. Lunneborg thus presents a picture of well-rounded people with the observed capacity for a wide range of human feeling and behaviour at work. One of the most surprising things to Lunneborg was the relish with which her sample took to managing and organising when the opportunity arose. Contrasting Friedan's different styles of managing,[57] Alpha or authoritarian/competitive and Beta, participative/cooperative, Lunneborg locates her women squarely within the Beta camp. They were 'relational, supportive, consensus building, tolerant of diversity and ambiguity, sharing and open to change' – as well as, let us not forget, competitive, ambitious and hardworking. In other words, Lunneborg, unlike Rosener, found *similarity as well as difference*, a point the literature on gender and business ethics would do well to take into account.

Lunneborg also notes, however, that men are sensing change and interpreting it as threatening, leaving open the possibility of backlash. These 'pioneering women' may be well placed and sufficiently experienced to survive a reaction, but if they are atypical then a backlash poses a serious threat, to the advancement of women's position in organisational life, and to equal opportunity generally.[58]

CONCLUDING COMMENTS

We hope that this chapter has brought some light to bear on the issue of gender and business ethics. As a relatively recent field of enquiry, it has made some progress; yet a number of questions remain unanswered and also unasked, leaving gaps in our understanding. Although much research effort, on which the literature on business ethics is building, has been directed to a search for *gender difference*, there is much to commend a complementary search for *similarity*. The discourse on gender and women's studies, which has developed largely independently of that on business ethics, has shown that there are similarities and differences between women and between men, as well as there being differences *and* similarities between women and men. At present the values of competition and

148

aggression rather than consensus and cooperation tend to pervade the power structures of organisational life, leading, as Burke *et al.*[59] suggest, to 'tough business attitudes' in the face of 'ethical niceties'. The former values are more commonly associated with men while the latter are connected with women. What the literature on gender and women's studies suggests is that we might search for a complementary balance.

Undoubtedly there remain considerable inequalities between women and men, evidenced by the persistence of sexual disadvantage and discrimination – and the wider structure of social, political and economic relationships which sustains this needs to be kept clearly in view. This poses a considerable challenge to the growing field of gender and business ethics, for rigorous research of both a psychological *and* a sociological kind which takes account of the complexities, not just of individuals and of gender, but of other socially structured levels of similarity and difference based on such factors as social class, ethnicity, age and religion. Once this exploration begins we will be in a far better position to understand the role of gender in business ethics, not as a single determining factor or dimension, but as part of the wider social reality that is organisational life.

NOTES

1 Horsman, M. (1995) 'What a week it was for . . . ad women: Smug advertising boys had better watch out', *Independent*, 17 March.
2 Drucker, Peter (1981) 'What is "Business Ethics"?', *The Public Interest*, 63, pp. 18–36.
3 For example, see Gellerman, S. W. (1986) 'Why Good Managers make Bad Ethical Choices', *Harvard Business Review*, July–Aug, 86(4), pp. 85–90; Cuilla, J. B. (1991) 'Why is Business Talking about Ethics?: Reflections on Foreign Conversations', *California Management Review*, Fall, pp. 67–86; Vogel, D. (1991) 'Business Ethics: New Perspectives on Old Problems', *California Management Review*, Summer, pp. 101–17.
4 Thompson, T. (1991) 'Managing Business Ethics', *Canadian Public Administration*, 34(1), Spring, pp. 153–7. See also Ruegger, D and King, E. W. (1992) 'A Study of the Effect of Age and Gender upon Student Business Ethics', *Journal of Business Ethics*, 11(3), pp. 179–86.
5 Sikula, A. Snr and Costa, A. D. (1994) 'Are Women more Ethical than Men?', *Journal of Business Ethics*, 13(11), pp. 859–71.
6 Cuilla, 'Why is Business Talking about Ethics?'
7 Mayer, D and Cava, A. (1993) 'Ethics and the Gender Equality

Dilemma for U.S. Multinationals', *Journal of Business Ethics*, 12(9), pp. 701–8.

8 Ibid., p. 704.

9 Cockburn, C. (1991) *In the Way of Women: Men's Resistance to Sex Equality in Organizations*, New York: Macmillan.

10 Cf: Bryan B., Dadzie, S. and Scafe, S. (1985) *The Heart of the Race – Black Women's Lives in Britain*, London: Virago.

11 Cf: Alcoff, L. (1988) 'Cultural Feminism versus Post-Structuralism: The Identity Crisis in Feminist Theory, Signs', *Journal of Women in Culture and Society*, 13(3), pp. 405–36.

12 Harris, J. R. (1989) 'Ethical Values and Decision Processes of Male and Female Business Students', *Journal of Education for Business*, vol. 8, pp. 234–38; see also Sikula and Costa, 'Are Women more Ethical than Men?'; Ruegger and King, 'A Study of the Effect of Age and Gender upon Student Business Ethics'.

13 Sikula and Costa, 'Are Women more Ethical than Men?'

14 Barnett J. H and Karson, M. J. (1989) 'Managers, Values and Executive Decisions: An Exploration of the Role of Gender, Career Stage, Organizational Level, Function and the Importance of Ethics, Relationships and Results in Managerial Decision-Making', *Journal of Business Ethics*, 8(10), pp. 747–71; quote is on p. 748.

15 Ibid.

16 Burke, T., Maddocks, S. and Rose, A. (1993) *How Ethical is British Business?: An Analysis of the Sensitivity of Senior Managers and Other Professionals to Ethical Issues in Business*, University of Westminster Research Working Paper, Series 2, No. 1.

17 Sikula and Costa, 'Are Women more Ethical than Men?'

18 Barnett and Karson, 'Managers, Values and Executive Decisions'.

19 Crow, S. M., Fok, L. Y., Hartman, S. and Payne, D. M. (1991) 'Gender and Values: What is the Impact on Decision Making?', *Sex Roles*, 25(3/4).

20 Harris, 'Ethical Values and Decision Processes of Male and Female Business Students'.

21 Galbraith, S. and Stephenson, H. B. (1993) 'Decision Rules used by Male and Female Students in Making Ethical Value Judgements: Another Look', *Journal of Business Ethics*, 12(3), pp. 227–33.

22 Ibid.

23 Goffee, R. (1993) 'Focus: Women in Management: An Empirical Exploration of Ethical Issues', *Business Ethics: A European Review*, 2(1), pp. 8–13; quote is on p. 12.

24 Galbraith and Stephenson, 'Decision Rules used by Male and Female Students in Making Ethical Value Judgements', p. 232.

25 Ruegger and King, 'A Study of the Effect of Age and Gender upon Student Business Ethics'.

26 Barnett and Karson, 'Managers, Values and Executive Decisions'.

27 Harris, 'Ethical Values and Decision Processes of Male and Female Business Students'.

28 Crow *et al.*, 'Gender and Values'.

29 Sikula and Costa, 'Are Women more Ethical than Men?', p. 870.

30 de Bruijn, J. (1993) 'Focus: Sex-Discrimination in Job Evaluation', *Business Ethics: A European Review*, 2(1), pp. 25–9.
31 Goffee, 'Focus: Women in Management'.
32 Davidson, M. J. and Cooper, C. L. (1992) *Shattering the Glass Ceiling: The Woman Manager*, London: Paul Chapman Publishing.
33 Coe, T. (1992) *The Key to the Men's Club: Opening the Doors to Women in Management*, Corby: The Institute of Management.
34 Cockburn, *In the Way of Women*.
35 Faludi, S. (1991) *Backlash – The Undeclared War against Women*, London: Chatto & Windus.
36 See Clarke, J. and Newmann, J. (1993) 'The Right to Manage: A Second Managerial Revolution?', *Cultural Studies*, 7(3), pp. 427–41. See also Newmann, J. (1994) 'The Limits of Management: Gender and the Politics of Change', in Clarke, J., Cochrane, A. and McLaughlin, E. (eds), *Managing Social Policy*, London: Sage.
37 Clark, H. (1991) *Women, Work and Stress: New Directions*, University of East London, *Occasional papers on Business, Economy and Society*, Paper No. 3.
38 Institute of Management (1994) *Fewer Women Managers*, press release, Corby: IOM.
39 Scarr, S. (1988) 'Race and Gender as Psychological Variables: Social and Ethical Issues', *American Psychologist*, 43(1), pp. 56–9.
40 Grimshaw, J. (1993) 'The Idea of a Female Ethic', in Singer, P. (ed.), *A Companion to Ethics*, Oxford: Blackwell, pp. 491–9.
41 Gilligan, C. (1982) *In a Different Voice: Psychological Theory and Women's Development*, Boston: Harvard University Press.
42 Barnett and Karson, 'Managers, Values and Executive Decisions'; Crow *et al.*, 'Gender and Values'.
43 Gilligan, *In a Different Voice*, p. 19.
44 Ibid., pp. 25–6.
45 Galbraith and Stephenson, 'Decision Rules used by Male and Female Students in Making Ethical Value Judgements'.
46 Benhabib, S. (1987) 'The Generalised and the Concrete Other', in Frazer, Elizabeth, Hornsby, Jennifer and Lovibond, Sabina (eds), *Ethics: A Feminist Reader*, Oxford: Blackwell; pp. 267–300.
47 Ibid., pp. 279, 283.
48 Ferguson, K. E. (1984) *The Feminist Case against Bureaucracy*, Philadelphia: Temple University Press; Rosener, J. B. (1990) 'Ways Women Lead', *Harvard Business Review*, vol. 90, Nov–Dec, pp. 119–25; Lunneborg, P. (1990) *Women–Changing–Work*, New York: Bergin & Garvey.
49 Burke *et al.*, *How Ethical is British Business?*
50 Ferguson, *The Feminist Case against Bureaucracy*.
51 Acker, J. (1990) 'Hierarchies, Jobs Bodies: A Theory of Gendered Organizations', *Gender and Society*, 4(2), pp. 139–58.
52 Burke *et al.*, *How Ethical is British Business?*, p. 24.
53 Rosener, 'Ways Women Lead'.
54 Lunneborg, *Women–Changing–Work*.
55 Ibid., p. xviii.

56 Kanter, R. M. (1977) *Men and Women of the Corporation*, New York: Basic Books/HarperCollins.
57 Friedan, B. (1981) *The Second Stage*, New York: Summit Books.
58 Lunneborg, *Women–Changing–Work*, p. 162.
59 Burke *et al.*, *How Ethical is British Business?*

12

PRIVATISED ETHICS

The case of the regulated utilities

Stephen Brigley and Peter Vass

INTRODUCTION

The ethics of privatised utilities has become an important social issue in the 1990s. Public disquiet in the UK has intensified as successive Conservative governments, prompted by an ideology of 'rolling back the State', have dismantled public service monopolies in transport and telecommunications, gas, water and electricity services. Production, transport and distribution networks have been sold off to the private sector, and 'surrogate' or direct competition introduced to approximate free market conditions. Only certain elements of 'natural' monopoly have survived the injection of competition into these public services.

Any debate about the ethics of the utilities has to recognise that privatisation remains ethically controversial. Water privatisation was rejected in Scotland on the grounds that public investment in water services and the benefits therefrom should be protected as a community inheritance. However, as privately owned utilities have become a fact of life, the focus of opposition has shifted. Social discomfort has been voiced about the loss of dependable and familiar service patterns (e.g. in rail transport) and the disappearance of symbols of national identity (e.g. red telephone boxes). More significant, perhaps, has been the growing public perception that some utility companies are making excessive profits, overpaying their directors and charging high prices, while giving an inadequate service to the consumer.

British Telecom, British Gas and the British Airports Authority (now BAA) were the network industries privatised first (1984, 1986 and 1987 respectively), but it has been the privatisation of the water and electricity industries (1989 onwards) and the restructuring and prospective privatisation of railways in 1996 which have been the focus for public concern over utility profits. Boardroom pay has been a public issue for them all, however, with Iain Vallance, Chairman of BT, criticised for suggesting to a Select Committee that junior hospital doctors had an easy life compared with him, and with the Board of British Gas being described by Ken Livingstone MP at its AGM, when concern over the remuneration of Cedric Brown, its chief executive, was at its height, as 'the most interesting thing to come to Docklands since the Kray twins'. The Conservative Energy Minister, Tim Eggar, even publicly appealed to the chairman of the National Grid company not to take his legal entitlement in the gain on share options when it was demerged from the regional electricity companies and listed on the Stock Exchange – all to no avail. Whether ministers should try to oblige directors to waive previous contractual agreements about the terms on which share options were granted – even if, with hindsight, they were mistaken – is itself an ethical issue. A further complicating factor is that public concern has been centred on the dramatic increases in the level of pay (to move from nationalised industry pay rates to those of comparable private sector companies), rather than on whether the absolute level itself is either too high or necessary to incentivise directors.

The UK debate on privatised utilities has been matched by an equally vigorous debate in the rest of the European Union, where strong forces are pushing for the breakdown of national monopoly provision in favour of liberalised utility services. These come in part from the legal requirements of the Treaty of Rome, which requires a common market in goods and services, and in part from business interests which see European competitiveness being eroded in comparison with the emerging 'tiger' economies of East Asia, and potentially Central and Eastern Europe. The latest pressure has been the desire of certain EU governments to achieve the convergence criteria for EMU. Opposing this, however, are public concerns about maintaining universal service obligations, reflected in calls for European Public Service Charters to be formally incorporated in the Act of European Union following the 1996 Inter-Governmental Conference.[1]

The period of privatisation in the UK has coincided with public concern about corporate governance and the ethics of business generally. This has steadily become more acute, and has widened to include the affairs of government and public administration, reflected in the deliberations of the Cadbury report; those of its successor committee, chaired by Sir Ronald Hampel of ICI; of the Greenbury report on boardroom pay; of the Select Committee on Employment looking specifically at regulated utilities;[2] and of Lord Nolan's committee investigating standards of executive behaviour in public bodies in the structurally reformed public sector. It is not surprising that the ethical standards of privatised utilities should also be questioned. However, the special invective reserved for these companies suggests that the public expects them to conform to 'higher' moral standards than those of private business.

Part of the purpose of this chapter is to examine the rationality and fairness of such criticisms. It will not be possible to do so, however, without first relating this ethics debate more clearly to theoretical frameworks of business ethics *per se*. Some preliminary examination of the evolving ethical perceptions of utilities' managements and key features of the context of their business will therefore be essential, before assessing the validity of popular views, and in applying theoretical insights.

PRIVATE SECTOR ETHICS

The change to private ownership of utilities, and a more competitive commercial environment, necessarily alters structures of corporate governance and stakeholder relationships. Boards of directors in the utilities have adopted a corporate approach, with traditional executive leadership by the CEO, and the counter-balancing influence of non-executive directors, replacing the bureaucratic link with the civil service and accountability to a government minister. Professional and other employee associations affected by privatisation often voice criticism of the values, goals and styles of public service managements. However, not all commentators see privatisation as a retrograde step for utilities' ethics. The principle of fair competition is frequently cited as the antidote to undesirable monopolistic practices, of which state-controlled public services are said to be a prime example. The ethical superiority of competitive markets is equated with:

- price levels equivalent to those needed to provide an economic return to efficient companies
- a choice of goods or services for consumers, recognising that there are different sections of market demand

- innovation and development of new processes, products, services and forms of business
- fair trade between sellers and purchasers, fair competition between sellers.[3]

The efficiency benefits which apparently flow from the disciplines of competition are precisely those which state-run utilities are supposed to inhibit.

Utilities which take the competitive principle seriously will perceive their moral and social responsibilities on the lines advocated by Friedman.[4] The limits of management decision-making are defined by free market economics, and ethical conduct appraised solely in terms of its contribution to company profitability. Friedman is ambiguous on whether the profit motive is entirely separate from ethical considerations or whether these factors are interdependent. Conformity to the law and conventional morality in Friedman's theory appears to imply a normative duty that business should operate without deception or fraud, but the *grounds* for this imperative are unclear. Is the justification again prudential, or based on some autonomous ethical value? Except for respect for property rights (of shareholders) and the free enterprise principle, executives are denied any other intrinsic ethical motivation. Managers who pursue ethical causes in their work ignore their duty to shareholders and unconscionably impose taxes on them without their consent. Ethics, on this view, is the sole responsibility of private individuals, and freedom is the right to non-interference, principles which Friedman sees as the only proper basis for a democratic society. Social interventions by governments will be necessary to correct externalities, inequalities and instabilities caused by competitive markets.

The nature of the corporation which matches the Friedmanite theory is defined by legal recognition: the corporation's creation as a legal entity simply recognises its existence as a freely constituted organisation, but involves it in no obligations to society other than those fulfilled by serving its own ends. This conception of the corporation is complemented by distinctive views of the duties of directors and managers. The relationship between shareholders and managers is one of principal–agent. Legal recognition narrowly defines the primary responsibilities of corporate management as those which serve the interests of the shareholders or 'owners' of the company: responsibilities to produce goods and services efficiently, to manage employees, company finances and resources, to innovate and adapt to new technologies and to guarantee corporate prosperity.[5] Thus, it is the *fiduciary relationship* of management to shareholders, limited possibly by the constraint of the takeover 'market', which governs what counts as an ethical motive and an ethical outcome in management decision-taking.

The perceived distorting effect of the profit motive on the ethical intentions of individuals and companies has led to attempts to replace the primacy of shareholders' interests with a stakeholder perspective.[6] This requires management to consider the interests of any group affected by the survival or prosperity of a corporation. A company's stakeholders may include not only shareholders, but also customers, suppliers, the community, employees and competitors. On this view, the corporation is a legal entity bound by a social contract which carries obligations to serve the social good and leaves open the possibility of state intervention to this end. Stakeholder theory promises a certain form of ethical improvement, commonly exemplified in corporate policies on employee welfare, environmental protection and customer care. However, it is a matter of debate whether the acceptance of responsibilities to a range of stakeholders will yield ethically optimal outcomes, and how proactive a company would have to be in order to fulfil its stakeholder duties.

The weighing of different stakeholder interests is fundamentally a utilitarian mechanism used in management decision-taking to ascertain the greater good. However, in order to work effectively, some trading-off of stakeholder *rights* appears to be unavoidable. But who is to say that the right of workers to have jobs in a local factory is more important than the right of local residents to breathe clean air? The cost of introducing anti-pollution equipment, while laudable, may ruin the company, destroy jobs and damage local communities. A Friedmanite may try to apply enlightened self-interest to such conflicts, but can ultimately retreat to upholding the shareholders' interests. Stakeholder theory, on the other hand, has no *prima facie* reason to prioritise a particular interest, so it can only resolve such conflicts of rights by opting for trade-offs. However, rights cannot be trumped by self-interest or by any aggregate of individual interests.[7] The appeal to rights itself invokes a greater good, but one which is grounded in universal concepts of human good and harm. Arguably, a public service ethic is required if rights claims are to be used as benchmarks to judge the ethics of the utilities.

PUBLIC SERVICE ETHICS

The ethics of public service generally assumes that access to what utilities provide is a universal right, and inequalities of provision are unjust. In a bold statement of this view, we find that:

> Everyone has the right of equal access to public services in his country.
> (UN Universal Declaration of Human Rights, Article 21(2))

Obviously it is too simplistic to assume that there is an absolute right to social resources. Nevertheless, the use of the language of rights in this context signals the importance of linking the benefits of utility provision to the common needs and capacities of human beings.[8]

The underpinning values of public service ethics are altruism, equality and the collective good. Public services should be concerned not only with economic and efficient provision to meet essential needs, but also with its equal distribution. They offer a service to the individual and the community rather than a vehicle for private profit. Given their special position in promoting the common good, the case for public regulation (or some form of central state planning) becomes compelling. Public services are expected to provide for the *whole* community, and therefore to enable a more stable and reliable infrastructure than is achievable by private enterprises in a free market economy.

Theoretically, the free market cannot guarantee pure public goods (such as national defence) because the rational self-interest of providers militates against bearing the costs of supply of a good for oneself which simultaneously will be available to all – far better to take the free rider option. Water, power, transport and telecoms are not perfect examples of public goods when judged by the criteria of indivisibility (when supplied to one person they are available to all) and non-excludability (consumption by one individual does not exclude others from consumption of the same). However, they may still be viewed as goods with positive externalities (i.e. they bring side-benefits to producers who have not paid for them), which implies a tendency for them to be under-produced in a free market economy.[9]

To meet the demands of public service ethics, a utility would be required to maintain universal service conditions. In an early statement of this commitment, the United States' Communications Act

(1934) justified government intervention in telecommunications by declaring its intention

> to make available, so far as possible, to all the people of the United States a rapid, efficient, nationwide and worldwide wire and radio communications service with adequate facilities at reasonable charges.[10]

Universal service conditions bring special benefits to the community:

- the maximisation of network conditions extends benefits of scale to all users
- the value of social cohesion is promoted in shared provision and a common quality of life
- the guarantee of individual access to what the utility provides fulfils a citizenship right

The practical ability of an unconstrained private sector to guarantee such benefits may be questioned. Private enterprises could choose to ignore long-term investment and the equitable distribution of services because of pressure to give a short-term return to shareholders. Moreover, their efforts to create universal service conditions will always be hindered by market failures and externalities. As a consequence the distribution and availability of a range of public goods could be uneven and irregular, both geographically and socially.

Because public services serve basic human needs, special social controls are imposed on them. Utilities' ethics, therefore, have to be interpreted within a statutory and regulatory environment which is designed to secure the public interest. However, the resulting ethical interface between government, the regulatory bodies, the courts and companies creates unusually complex conditions for the mediation of the public interest. This is compounded in democratic societies by difficult issues of accountability, participation and representation which are not always understood by the utilities' detractors.

REGULATION: THE PUBLIC/PRIVATE DIVIDE

The very nature of the utilities' business creates an ambiguous context which cannot be ignored in the assessment of their ethics. The utilities mediate the private and the public interest, the individual and the collective good. In that sense they may be expected to partake of private sector and public service ethics. On the one hand, utilities' executives find that, unlike other private sector companies, their business freedom is constrained by regulators, each of whom is accountable to a particular government minister, and then to Parliament and the relevant Select Committee of the House of Commons. The regulator brings pricing, supply and quality of service into line with competitive models, and generally ensures conditions of public accountability. On the other hand, privatisation has bred a more enterprising style of management with direct accountability to shareholders (probably a wider cross-section of society than previously). Competition from both national and foreign companies has focused the minds of utilities' managers more than ever on economy, efficiency and profit.

Public expectations about the utilities have clearly been conditioned by the post-war consensus on the public/private sector divide. Utilities, or network industries, are traditionally publicly owned. One major reason is that some of their functions, the provision of pipes and wires, are natural monopolies because of strong economies of scale, and competing networks would be inefficient and wasteful. If they are to be privatised, then this must be accompanied by public regulation, which has been the case. Regulation has been carried out by independent regulators with their own non-ministerial public body (e.g. OFWAT – the Office of Water Services, and OFFER – the Office of Electricity Regulation).

The public has not been sympathetic to the regulated industries as the post-privatisation record has unfolded. Yet directors of the companies might reasonably argue that their approach to managing the privatised utilities is fully consistent with the democratic intention of Parliament when privatising the industries and setting up the regulatory regime, and that their position is, therefore, ethically secure. In addition, they can point to the real record in many cases of improving efficiency, falling prices and rising standards. Why, they then ask, are we so unjustly accused and poorly judged?

Two key factors have to be taken into account. First, the utilities are not perceived as typical private companies, simply because they have been privatised. They are seen as providing essential public services and, therefore, are an intermediate set of industries between public ownership with public accountability and private ownership in a competitive marketplace, owing no necessary accountability to people other than the owners. In effect, the context is one of public services, albeit privately provided. Second, public understanding of the sophisticated regulatory system is low and, therefore, judgements about the performance of the industries and the behaviour of the directors may be made with reference to the wrong benchmarks and criteria. For these reasons, the debate about ethical management in utilities may have been distorted by a failure of both public presentation by the companies concerning their public service mission (which should be clearly distinguished from diversification into non-regulated, non-public service activities) and public communication by the government, regulators and companies about the fundamentals of the regulatory system to a wide public.

To illustrate the latter, we can compare annual profit or rate of return regulation with the incentive-based, price control system which is used to regulate utilities in the UK. Rate of return regulation as traditionally used in the USA to control private utilities means that excess profits are not (apparently) earned. By definition, therefore, there is no public concern about private profit from public service. However, the industries have no financial incentive to efficiency, and while the public service ethic of doing a good job for its own sake *might* be sufficient to achieve an efficient outcome, the experience of inefficient nationalised industries and privately owned utilities under rate of return regulation appears to show it doesn't happen in practice (which is a separate and important research question about the incentive properties of the public service ethic in practice).

A fixed price control for a period, however, gives the incentive for directors to improve on the expenditure forecasts on which the regulator has based the price controls. If this can be achieved, then excess profit (alternatively known as economic profit) can be earned until the regulator reviews the price cap. At that point (typically every five years) the regulator can pass on the benefit of the efficiency improvements which have been 'revealed' by the company because of the financial incentives to customers by way of lower prices. In this system, higher profits are, therefore, the *quid pro quo* for lower prices in the long run, and it might, therefore, be judged reasonably ethical to say that 'high utility profits are not necessarily a bad thing for the consumer'.

Two recent examples demonstrate, however, that awareness of the fundamentals of the regulatory system is not informing the public in their judgment on utilities and their directors. First, the severe drought in 1995 caused water restrictions, particularly in Yorkshire. It has always been the basis of public investment that capacity and water resources were not provided to meet supply in all circumstances, no matter how severe the circumstances. The public would cooperate with a community spirit in rationing in such extreme circumstances, and occasional restrictions are built into the regulatory standards for deciding allowable expenditure and price controls.[11] The public reaction to restrictions in 1995, however, was very adverse, notwithstanding the facts about the exceptional drought; conditioned by the view that illegitimate profits were being earned and, if so, customers expected private companies to deliver the goods and services they offer.

Second, there was public concern over the electricity regulator's proposals for price controls on the electricity distribution businesses announced in 1994. The subsequent attempt by Trafalgar House to take over Northern Electricity, one of the regional electricity companies, led to more information being revealed by the company's directors in their defence. In the light of this[12] and other factors,[13] proposals were tightened by the regulator, but the public was left with the impression that the electricity companies had not been honest with the regulator in the way in which a nationalised industry board would have been expected to be with its minister. The fact that the incentive regulatory system is necessarily based on an adversarial relationship between the company (if it is accepted that financial rewards are necessary to 'incentivise' utility managers) and the regulator, who is acting as a 'surrogate' for competition, appears to have had no impact on ameliorating the public's judgment. The surrogate role itself confuses the public, which interprets the regulator as balancing the interests of the company with those of the customer, rather than seeing the primary objective of regulation as customer protection, which is in fact the case. From this emanates a rather misguided debate on whether consumers should be represented independently from the regulatory offices.[14]

PRIVATISED ETHICS: EARLY INDICATORS

In the case of the utilities, an open-ended prospect may be inferred: government and regulators, industry-specific factors, individual managers and boards, traditional and emergent organisational cultures, and employees', consumers' and professional groups may combine to create distinctive positions on ethics. Whatever the outcomes, one thing is certain: *denationalisation and fragmentation of public services have shifted responsibility for ethical behaviour in the utilities to individual companies and their executives.* Within the complex ethical interface between government, the regulator and the utilities, we can expect boards of directors to be key players in evolving corporate ethical values and practices.

Preliminary insights into the ethical assumptions of the utilities' boards about the balance between private and public sector ethics have been drawn from the present authors' 1994–5 survey of the chairmen of UK regulated utilities. The survey covered the UK electricity industry, water companies in England and Wales, British Gas, BT and BAA. Twenty chairmen responded out of fifty in total (40 per cent) but, because of the high proportion of the smaller water-only companies in the population (twenty-one), the responses, in fact, cover a large majority of the regulated assets and associated turnover.

The results suggest that ethical conduct has a significant place on the agendas of utilities' boards. While only 30 per cent of companies had an explicit code of ethics, ethical statements were included in the vast majority of other public documents, such as annual reports. Most companies (75 per cent) included ethics in staff induction or management training programmes, and the chairmen reported that 95 per cent of companies had discussed ethical practice at board meetings (35 per cent on more than five occasions) and that 90 per cent had discussed ethics in general terms, not simply in relation to specific issues or situations. Most significantly, 80 per cent expected their company to be actively increasing its staff awareness of ethics in the near future. Comments such as 'we are currently reviewing the area of business ethics and plan to develop a new code of business ethics for our business' show that we can expect an increase in the number of explicit codes. However, one chairman did report that, while there was no explicit code, 'ethical standards had been implicit for over 100 years'. Also, staff know that 'any suggestion of unfairness to a customer will be followed up by me'. Alternatively, another reported that 'the public benefit gets submerged in commercial games'. These responses indicate the need for empirical research to describe and investigate how these perceptions of continuity and change in corporate ethics are expressed in the ethical performance of the companies.

The responses to our four positioning statements (see Table 12.1) were also very revealing, and indicate on balance that utility managements do consider that their ethical position is to act in accordance with private sector practice, given an incentive-based regulatory system which publicly rationalises and controls the privatised utilities' monopoly power on behalf of the public and consumers.

Ninety-five per cent of the chairmen reported that they thought their Board of Directors as a whole would generally agree with their responses; and similarly so for their employees. This interesting response warrants further inquiry into intra-company ethical perceptions.[15]

Table 12.1 Ethical positioning of chairmen of the privatised utilities

Statement	Strongly Agree	Agree	Disagree	Strongly Disagree
1 The ethics of managing a regulated company should be the same as those of managing any private sector company.	40%	45%	15%	–
2 The regulatory system and the statutory framework should establish the social obligations to be met by regulated companies.	15%	35%	40%	10%
3 Regulated companies should have no special obligation to help the regulators achieve their objectives, other than meeting specified statutory regulatory requirements.	20%	60%	20%	–
4 The term 'public service' means the same as 'customer care'.	10%	15%	70%	5%

DISCUSSION

The deeply entrenched public perception of utilities as 'public services, privately provided', and the mismatch between the public's and directors' criteria for judging utility management's behaviour, are only likely to be resolved in the short run with the introduction of catalysts which inspire public debate and understanding of the unique position of regulated utilities. Ultimately, it will only be possible to judge properly the ethical behaviour of utility companies' directors if there is a clear understanding and consensus around the objectives, context and role of regulation as 'surrogate' competition. Regulation is intended to replicate the equivalence of prices and consumer choice in a competitive market and to act as a counter-balance to undesirable monopolistic tendencies in the public services. Our survey indicates that directors generally subscribe to this interpretation of the regulatory role and see themselves as actors in the surrogate competitive context. This position is ethically defensible if the basic premises of 'incentive' regulation by independent public regulators are accepted.

There is also evidence in the survey that the standards of ethical conduct and corporate governance of a regulated utility are perceived as no different from those of any other company. Thus, the accepted view of regulation does not imply any diminution in the responsibility of directors, either individually or collectively, to act ethically. *If the public service ethic is no longer in vogue, then the adoption of a stakeholder model rather than Friedmanite ethics seems more likely, as utilities' directors seek to meet their corporate responsibilities.* The wider concept of the 'stakeholder economy', currently being discussed and actively adopted by New Labour, may stimulate a wider examination of how the present system can reconcile public service with private provision. However, it is important that residual elements of public service ethics should not be obscured by utilitarian logic.

Ethical tensions arise when private sector economic disciplines require reductions in services. In a recent case, a railway station regularly used by a disabled person was closed. Transit to the nearest alternative station prolonged the journey so much as to make it pointless for this individual. Reduction of rail services will serve certain stakeholders (e.g. the shareholders and those employees who keep their jobs), but not others. This is an example of the kind of trade-off which is unacceptable if equality of access to provision is

165

a social right. Similar questions of justice and rights underpin the policies of utility companies towards non-payers. Whether to disconnect non-paying customers (or to introduce self-disconnection through metering), and how to discriminate between those who cannot pay and those unwilling to pay, are issues which are difficult to handle using the stakeholder model. A utilitarian approach may yield undesirable side effects: the magnification of inequalities of access and social need, and the creation of an underclass effectively excluded from full participation in citizenship.

It was argued above that the public service model prioritises network conditions and reasonable access to public services for all sections of society. However, the problem of uneconomic costs in the delivery of public services complicates the simple right of equal access with considerations of just and efficient pricing.[16] Obviously, delivering a letter to the Orkney Islands costs more than delivering one to Central London. Since the charge is the same for all users, postal services to and from the Orkney Islands receive a hidden subsidy. The traditional use of cross-subsidies was one way to keep a just balance among such costs, but now the tariff has to reflect the actual cost of supply. The increasing transparency of the policy environment may generate proposals for discriminatory pricing, but this would only raise further issues of equality and the individual's ability to pay.

Of special ethical concern are the negative externalities associated with the utilities. Their extensive network industries leave hardly any part of the environment untouched, with land, air and water pollution, noise and unsightly plant and transmission networks all having an adverse impact. Moreover, the success or failure of the utilities has a profound effect upon public health and the social well-being of the nation, not to mention its economic base. One unintended outcome of privatisation could be a weakening of social cohesion. National utilities may have had a place in the public consciousness on a par with that of the National Health Service. The national identities of traditional public services have been superseded under privatisation by corporate identities (though regional titles tend to be retained by some water, electricity and gas companies). However, the loss of household names such as 'British Rail' and 'British Gas', along with their traditional symbols of identity, may seem a small price to pay for a more efficient service.

Once again, it may be argued that the externalities problem is the same for the utility company as for any other major corporation

(ICI, for example). However, there is a crucial difference in account-ability. The mainstream private sector company can feel reasonably satisfied with a reactive approach to its moral and social responsi-bilities (i.e. the observation of negative moral prohibitions). A util-ity company cannot afford to be other than proactive on corporate ethics (it must be governed by Kantian 'imperfect' duties). The expectation that the utilities deliver on issues of equality, justice and the general good is epitomised in the corporate policies of France's national electricity utility.[17] It amounts to the claim that in ethical terms they must not only act *responsibly* towards stakeholders, but make themselves publicly *accountable* for their positive achieve-ments in those areas.

CONCLUSION

The end-point of this discussion brings us back to the legal and reg-ulatory framework: can it be expected to bear the additional burden of calling the utilities to account for their performance on ethics? The regulator as a surrogate for competition cannot be equated with an impersonal market mechanism. Intervention by the regula-tor in the utilities market is not a neutral event, notwithstanding the disavowals in early OFTEL annual reports of any responsibility for the public interest. The normative aspect of regulation was dis-played in legally enforced investigations by the regulator to ascer-tain that supply and quality standards were maintained by South West Water in 1995. However, any strengthening of the normative framework by statute would need to be accompanied by supportive measures.

Effective regulation for public accountability requires the *eco-nomic* regulator to be supported by a *quality* regulator responsible for putting constraints in the system for areas such as quality, health and safety, the correction of negative externalities (using instru-ments such as command and control, market signals through tax rates and tradeable permits). The judicious introduction of regula-tory penalties and incentives could press the utilities to be proactive on social and distributional matters. Moreover, a recasting of the legal obligations of regulators would demonstrate clearly the central objective of customer protection and facilitate a better public understanding of the nature and benefit of incentive regulation for privatised utilities.

A further step towards regulatory reform would be the acceleration of profit sharing, while leaving the long-run value of the financial incentive for companies intact (on lines proposed by the present Water Regulator, Ian Byatt). Reforms of corporate governance could complement external and internal pressures for utilities' directors to demonstrate moral responsibility. One stakeholder-based proposal is to bind directors by a duty of trusteeship rather than the principal–agent relationship: their role would be to 'balance fairly the various claims to the returns which (company) assets generate'.[18] Such reforms, once again, could assist utilities' directors to gain popular legitimacy.

Privatisation has so changed the ethical context of the utilities' business that it is unrealistic to expect a reinstatement of ethics based in rational cooperation for the public good. As long as regulators act mainly as 'surrogates' for competition, utilities' directors will continue to treat them as adversaries, and companies will erect walls of confidentiality and secrecy around their business at the expense of openness and transparency. On such points the mixed system of private enterprises providing public services is at its most contradictory. These contradictions cannot be easily resolved. The capacity of regulation alone to protect consumers and the public interest is surely limited. It may be necessary, given the strength of public opinion, to triangulate consumer empowerment[19] with changes in the regulatory framework and corporate governance, if we are to see a revival of social consensus around the public–private ethics divide.

NOTES

1 European Centre of Enterprises With Public Participation (1995) *Europe, Competition and Public Service*, Brussels: CEEP.
2 House of Commons Employment Committee (1995) *The Remuneration of Directors and Chief Executives of Privatised Utilities*, Third Report, HC 159, 27 June, London: HMSO.
3 Knight, A (1974) *Private Enterprise and Public Intervention: The Courtaulds Experience*, London: George Allen & Unwin, pp. 203–4.
4 Friedman, M. (1970) 'The Social Responsibility of Business is to Increase its Profits', *New York Times Magazine*, 13 September, pp. 32–4, 122–6.
5 Boatright, J. R. (1993) *Ethics and the Conduct of Business*, Englewood Cliffs, NJ: Prentice-Hall.
6 Evan, W. and Freeman, R. (1995) 'A Stakeholder Theory of the Modern Corporation: Kantian Capitalism', in Hoffman, M. and

Frederick, R. (eds), *Business Ethics: Readings and Cases in Corporate Morality*, 3rd edn, New York: McGraw-Hill, pp. 145–154.

7 Dworkin, R. M. (1978) *Taking Rights Seriously*, London: Duckworth.

8 Almond, B. (1991) 'Rights', in Singer, P. (ed.), *A Companion to Ethics*, Oxford: Blackwell, pp. 259–69.

9 Haslett, D. W. (1994) *Capitalism with Morality*, Oxford: Clarendon Press.

10 Quoted from Vietor, R. H. K. (1989) *Strategic Management and the Regulatory Environment: Cases and Industry Notes*, Englewood Cliffs, NJ: Prentice-Hall, p. 282.

11 OFWAT (1995) *Report on the levels of service for the water industry in England and Wales 1994–5*, November, Birmingham.

12 OFFER. (1995) *The Distribution Price Controls: Revised Proposals*, July, Birmingham.

13 Monopolies and Mergers Commission (1995) *Scottish Hydro-Electric Plc*, May, London: HMSO.

14 Vass, P. (1995) 'Consumer Representation – Integration or Independence?', *Regulatory Review*, London: Centre for the Study of Regulated Industries (CRI), CIPFA, pp. 225–37.

15 The divergence between commercial and public-service perceptions, for example, is a strong theme in Goodwin, B. (1995) *Perceptions of Moral Responsibility and Ethical Questions: A Study of a Water Company*, Henley Management College, Working Paper Series, Henley-on-Thames.

16 Argondona, A. (1994) 'Business, Law and Regulation: Ethical Issues', in Harvey, B. (ed.), *Business Ethics: A European Approach*, London: Prentice-Hall International, pp. 124–53.

17 Donaldson, J. (1992) *Business Ethics: A European Casebook*, London: Academic Press.

18 Kay, J. and Silberston, A. (1995) 'Corporate Governance', *National Institute Economic Review*, August, pp. 84–97.

19 Craig-Smith, N. (1990) *Morality and the Market: Consumer Pressure for Corporate Accountability*, London: Routledge.

13

TRADE UNIONS AND ETHICS
Unions as agents
Patrick Flood and Philip Stiles

INTRODUCTION

There has been considerable debate recently about the continuing viability of trade unions as labour market institutions. Unions in Western economies have sustained a haemorrhaging of members in recent years internationally, particularly in the private sector. This loss of membership, arising from a mixture of business cycle effects, structural factors, governmental and employer strategies, has potentially important implications for ethical behaviour within organisations.

In this chapter, we examine one major question arising from this situation, namely: what are the dangers inherent in an organisational environment where managerial behaviour is unconstrained by union presence? The discussion, therefore, investigates the potential positive contribution of unions as a regulatory ethical (and economic) mechanism.

Unions are important mechanisms in helping to achieve fairness within organisations, specifically in terms of the contract between employer and employee.[1] Because individual workers are in a weak negotiating position with respect to management, it is advantageous for workers to unite in order to reduce the power asymmetry. Discussions on the ethics of union activity have usually centred largely around such issues as the right to strike, the use of the closed shop, the political nature of unions, and problems of shirking, featherbedding, and resistance to change. These issues are familiar and the ethical arguments have been well discussed.[2] In this chapter, we shall look first at one persistent and influential criticism of trade unions: that they act as labour monopolies and, as monopolies, are unethical because they operate forms of restrictive practice.[3] This criticism was forcefully made by Freeman and Medoff[4] in their famous description of 'the two faces of unionism'. The alternative face to the monopoly view in this work is the 'Collective Voice/Institutional Response' view, which argues that unions have beneficial economic effects, increasing the morale of workers by creating equitable and safe working arrangements, protecting workers against arbitrary employer action. In the main body of the chapter, we shall argue that the monopoly view of trade unions bears little resemblance to reality and that the unions' role in expressing employee voice acts as a useful mechanism in reducing agency conflicts with respect to employers.

MONOPOLY POWER

Some economists view trade unions essentially as labour monopolies willing and capable of raising their members' wages in excess of unorganised workers in the same industry, through the use of techniques such as inflexible working practices and the strike weapon, in a fashion which rarely takes account of the – albeit sometimes nebulous – public interest. This mark-up, it is argued, is detrimental to economic efficiency, leading to reductions in output levels and ultimately to employment losses.

Such a line of argument typically also highlights cases involving undemocratic decision-making within trade unions, exemplified by instances of unions taking strike action without the support of their members. Viewed thus, trade unions and their actions in a normative sense might be viewed as unethical creations, and out of step with the needs of the much vaunted 'enterprise culture'.

However, trade unions differ from monopolistic firms in several important ways. Monopolistic firms set prices to maximise profits. Trade unions, by contrast, *bargain* over wages with employers. Further, successful wage bargaining by unions may cause employers to reduce employment. Thus, the maximising view of trade unions is likely to be an unrealistic assumption because of the wage–employment trade-off which trade unions regularly face. While a monopolistic firm's sole goal is to maximise profits, the trade union must grapple with a complex internal decision process revolving around its members' objectives in terms of long-term job security and short-term wage increases.

If trade unions were to raise wages above competitive levels then the associated higher costs of production incurred by the firms involved would in fact lead to employment reductions and the erosion of the trade union itself. The organisation of the entire industry by the relevant union, while likely to reduce output and employment levels of that sector, would safeguard the survival of the unionised firms in that sector. Further, there are industry sectors where firms possess different cost structures associated with barriers to entry and economies of scale and scope. Where unions organise those firms with the lowest costs of production, they are able to raise wages without fear of destroying such firms. Thus, even those ideologically committed to the monopolistic union perspective face important qualifications to their arguments.

The monopoly view of unions also seems detached from data on union influence. The election of the Thatcher government in 1979, the recession of the 1980s and high levels of unemployment, have resulted in a shift of power away from unions.[5] As Milner states,[6] the late 1980s saw the proportion of employees who have their pay and conditions affected by collective pay-setting institutions fall to below 50 per cent, and 'the abolition of the remaining wages councils in 1993 means that, for the first time in five decades, more than 50 per cent of employees have neither a legal minimum floor to their wages nor a union to negotiate on their behalf over their pay'. Purcell's comments[7] on the 'end of institutional industrial relations' reflect the sharp decline in union presence since 1979, with aggregate union membership falling from 13.2 million in 1980 to 9.9 million by 1990; and union density falling from 54 per cent to 38 per cent.[8] Unemployment persists at around 8–9 per cent, reducing the prospects for union growth, and unions have had to face serious problems concerning financial resources.[9] The general picture, therefore, seems to be one of serious decline in union influence. What are the moral implications of such a decline?

COLLECTIVE VOICE: THE UNION AS AGENT

The most obvious concern, both practically and morally, arising from the loss of union influence is that managerial behaviour may become unconstrained. Two central perspectives on the workings of organisations are agency theory and transaction theory, which both view the firm as a nexus of contracts. A major focus of recent research in organisational theory has been to ensure that contracting parties do not behave in an opportunistic, self-interested fashion towards one another, and to ensure that the interests of each are served. The relationship between the employer and the union may be viewed as a particular case of the principal–agent relationship, a relationship which, according to agency theory, gives rise to partial goal conflict. There is thus a moral hazard within such a relationship, which can occur on both sides of the contracting parties. The literature is replete with discussions of employee shirking, absenteeism, pilfering and so on. Workers are expected to do a 'fair day's work for a fair day's pay', and this is a moral obligation.[10] But often neglected is the problem of the employer shirking its responsibilities to the contract with its employees – for example, by such practices as arbitrary sackings, low wages, neglect of workplace health and safety conditions, misuse of employee pension funds, and so on. There is a moral obligation on management to engage in fair employment practices, which, as De George states, 'include following equitable guidelines and not discriminating on the basis of sex, race, religion, or other non-job-related characteristics'. The union, as agent, can act to nullify such malfeasance or opportunistic behaviour, using the collective might of its members to reduce the asymmetry in power between the parties. According to Faith and Reid[11] there are three ways a union can achieve this:

1 by providing its members with labour market information and aiding in contract negotiation with the firm
2 by monitoring and controlling the fulfilment of the contract between union members and the employer
3 by providing an outlet for employee voice

Employees typically look to unions to provide some, or all, of these benefits.[12] The first service allows individual employees an opportunity to determine their current market value and assess the appropriateness of their compensation contract; the second provides a governance service in order to determine deviance from features of the original contract of employment; the third is particularly important in larger firms where there is less contact between employees and management. This service is well known from the classic writings of Freeman and Medoff.[13] They argue that social actors within institutional settings, when confronted with social and economic problems, have two basic options – exit and voice. Faced with an unacceptable set of social or economic situations, consumers can choose to exit the relationship (e.g dissatisfied consumers choose another brand of product, dissatisfied employees quits his/her job). In a labour market setting, quitting is analogous to exit behaviour in that good employees penalise bad employers by joining another firm, which benefits the new employer, and economic efficiency in general, by eventually squeezing out bad employers who are depleted by the drain on their productive base of human capital. In a freely competitive market, liberal economists argue that the entry–exit mechanism is a sufficient arbitrage mechanism to resolve such situations.

Another mechanism is, of course, giving 'voice' – discussing problems, raising complaints, threatening to exit the relationship, bargaining in order to effect changes in the basic nature of the relationship. Rather than exiting, the aggrieved party seeks redress within the existing relationship in order to improve it. Trade unions provide a collective voice mechanism for employees which is backed by the 'muscle' afforded by the capacity, if necessary, to withdraw labour through the strike weapon. Because of the capacity of the union to prevent individual victimisation as a result of giving voice, dissatisfied employees are more likely to air grievances without fear of retribution.

Following this line of reasoning, Freeman and Medoff[14] postulated a number of reasons why unions may enhance productivity, and many of these arguments still have force. Their main argument is that unions lock workers into jobs by gaining better pay and conditions for them. Thus, turnover of experienced workers is reduced, speed and quality can be more easily maintained, and waste is kept to a minimum. Other points put forward include such arguments as:

- unions, through a 'shock' effect, smarten up management
- better communication channels enable workers to suggest improved ways of doing things
- the better morale of unionized workers improves their performance

From the perspective of employers, also, the benefit of having unions as agents in the workplace is clear. Employees' perception that employers are opportunist or malfeasant is likely to cause turnover and reluctance to learn firm-specific skills. To become an employer of choice, therefore, some firms may welcome the presence of an independent monitor of firm behaviour towards employees. The cost advantages of dealing with a single agent in contract transactions is also a powerful lever of union influence.[15]

IS NON-UNIONISM BAD FOR EMPLOYEES?

Recent evidence from the British Workplace Industrial Relations surveys (WIRS)[16] suggests that employees in the non-union private sector are at a considerable disadvantage when compared with their unionised private sector counterparts. Non-union employees in Britain receive, on average, much less information from management, are provided with fewer information/communication channels, and work in organisations with fewer health and safety representatives than their unionised counterparts. Further analyses indicate that non-union private sector workplaces (when compared with unionised private sector workplaces) experience higher accident and injury rates, more dismissals of a non-redundancy nature, and provide fewer grievance and disciplinary procedures to their employees. In addition, non-union workplaces experience more compulsory redundancies, higher levels of labour turnover, but virtually no strikes. Absenteeism levels within non-union firms were viewed by survey respondents to be as good as those for their unionised counterparts.

While the climate of employee relations was seen by managers to be good in non-union workplaces, issues of 'morale' were seen as problematic, associated perhaps with the labour turnover problem cited earlier. Pay comparisons reveal an interesting picture; the non-union companies in the private sector record greater pay dispersion and a higher incidence of low pay. Pay is more often performance related and determined by market forces than in the unionised private sector. Non-union workplaces also record higher usage levels of contingent workers and fewer personnel specialists than their unionised counterparts. The picture painted by the British WIRS data suggests that there is a real danger that unorganised workers can expect more informal but much less favourable institutional arrangements for 'voice' and 'due process' than workers employed in unionised private sector workplaces.

One can see that non-unionism confers (in the British private sector context), considerable 'freedom to manoeuvre' upon employers in terms of their employee relations strategies and in terms of organising more flexible working arrangements. However, from the perspective of these employees, greater flexibility in working arrangements does not translate into higher wages or more favourable working conditions. This is good news for British trade unions faced with a continuing debate about their relevance to a modern dynamic economy.

Interestingly, the WIRS data also raises some policy questions for would-be labour law legislators. If unions do not organise in currently unorganised private sector workplaces, what governance arrangements need to be legislated for in order to prevent the potential exploitation of non-union employees? This debate is currently rife in the United States. Defenders of non-union approaches, of course, can argue that the WIRS data on non-union companies is size-related, deriving from the fact that non-union workplaces are typically smaller and that many of them are independent, in the sense that they do not belong to part of a larger enterprise.

Based on this evidence, the highly visible and proactive human resource strategies deployed by companies such as Marks & Spencer, IBM and others must, at least in the British context, be regarded as 'atypical'. This is not a trivial point, as much of the laudatory literature on non-unionism has, until recently, had a narrow empirical base from which to extrapolate.

UNIONISM AND NEW MANAGEMENT TECHNIQUES

The decline in union influence, whether permanent or temporary, has for the present given management the upper hand. There is evidence, however, that this decline is not the result of any concerted management effort against union activity, but rather that the traditional sites of union activity and membership – for example, large manufacturing operations – have been cut back or closed, and there has been a strong sectoral shift in the economy towards service-based industries, which are typically much less unionised.[17] Nevertheless, there are a number of challenges which face trade unions from what has come to be called 'the new industrial relations'. These may range from aggressively anti-union stances (the employment of 'union-busting' practices), through union substitution approaches, towards full-blown human resource management (HRM).[18]

The first case normally involves the derecognition of weak unions, but it is a comparatively rare occurrence in established organisations, though prominent examples include GCHQ, the government's communications centre, parts of the printing industry and shipping.[19] It is rare because, as we have noted, unions provide value to employers by allowing employees voice, and also because to derecognise unions implies that alternative procedures for resolving grievances, and for negotiating pay and conditions are in place, which may prove highly problematic, particularly in large firms. However, when acquisitions are made or new sites opened, some firms exclude union membership, an example being the London Docklands Light Railway in the mid-1980s when it was an operating subsidiary of London Transport.[20] Partial derecognition is thus a more common phenomenon than total derecognition. As Gregg and Yates state, '13 per cent of companies with recognised unions in 1984 had at least partial derecognition by 1990'.[21] Collective representation has also been undermined by the growing practice of placing individual employees, particularly in management grades, on personal contracts, thus reducing the need for collective arrangements.

The move to marginalise trade unions is a feature of many descriptions of HRM. Though there are differing normative and conceptual models, some fuzziness over the distinction between HRM and personnel management, and the distinct gap between the rhetoric and reality of human resource processes and practices, the heart of HRM is usually taken to include:

- integrating HRM with organisational goals
- locating HRM in line management
- emphasising the link between the individual and the organisation rather than bargaining through collective procedures.[22]

One of the underlying values of HRM is the denial of pluralism, with the assumption that there are no differences of interest between management and employees.[23] There has, therefore, been much debate over whether HRM and trade union activity are compatible. The evidence points to the fact that HRM and trade unions do coexist[24] but, as Guest argues, the main path to improved performance 'is likely to require a shift in emphasis away from the industrial relations system towards HRM policies. . . .'[25]

HRM places strong emphasis on the competence and quality of management, and it could be argued that high quality management would be less likely to operate in an opportunistic or malfeasant manner. The need for unions to act as agents for employees would appear, therefore, to be minimal in such circumstances. The threat posed by HRM and other new management techniques has led to some refocusing in the trade union movement. Two task forces set up by the Trades Union Congress (TUC) looked at HRM and employee representation. The first urged that HRM should not be ignored if unions are to have any influence in the workplace, and the second looked to the European directives to establish rights for workplace information and consultation, through employee-based works councils and union membership.[26]

A number of commentators have seen this as a backward step by the TUC. As Kelly states, 'some in the trade union movement are rightly alarmed at this defeatist retreat from full bargaining rights and independent trade unionism, and dismayed by the associated rhetoric of class collaboration (or 'social partnership' as it is now called)'.[27]

The main issue here is that the initiatives designed to substitute for unionism (e.g. HRM) or to dilute the influence of unions (e.g. consultation, rather than full bargaining rights) are employer-led. HRM has been increasingly identified, not only as a unitarist doctrine, but also an instrumental one, treating employees as resources much like any other resource (the so-called 'hard' HRM school), emphasising efficiency and productivity but largely ignoring the quality of working life.[28] This is particularly clear in organisations which use a Just In Time system, or other elements of a Japanese-style workplace. As Delbridge and Turnbull state:

> the practices of teamwork, quality consciousness and flexibility which characterise such HRM strategies are in essence the means by which the workforce is controlled, through a mixture of stress, peer pressure, surveillance and accountability. Moreover, this style of HRM facilitates the regulation of work through the employment of a standardised workforce which is ultimately forced to conform to managerial requirements.[29]

The loss of independence implied in unions adopting partnership style approaches with employers is a serious concern, and whether there can be equality between employer and employee in a non-union setting, with all the power and information asymmetries involved, is a moot point.[30] Even if social partnership is a sensible way to move forward, there is no legal support for it, which makes the prospect of employers adopting it very slight.[31]

EMPLOYEE REPRESENTATION

Our analysis to date suggests that trade unions do have an important regulatory impact on the ethical behaviour of managers. The next question we must address, therefore, is the issue of how best to institutionalise this beneficial aspect of trade unions. The clearest form of institutionalisation of trade unions within organisations is for board level participation. As Parkinson states, 'for employee involvement to be able to influence enterprise policy it must be at the highest level in the organisation and at other points at which strategic decisions are made'.[32]

There has been little desire on the part of UK companies to introduce worker representatives on to the board (not only through fear of union influence but also through suspicion that representation may be a key step on the path to introducing two-tier boards). The Committee of Inquiry on Industrial Democracy (the Bullock Report) of 1975, which recommended employee representation on the board of firms with over 2000 employees, and the EC Fifth Directive on the Harmonisation of Company Law in the European Community (last amended in 1989), which offers a number of employee participation scenarios, have been actively opposed by large UK companies and stifled by a lack of political will.[33]

Union ambitions have also been rather limited, due in part to their diminishing power base and also (on the part of some) to an ideological aversion to sharing decision-making with the managers of capital. However, despite these practical limitations, are there convincing theoretical arguments for board-level representation of employees?

The experience of worker directors on the supervisory boards of German corporations has had a largely positive impact on German industry. This derives in part from its mandatory status under German law which sharply distinguishes it from the UK and US schemes which are voluntary in emphasis. Partly reflecting this lack of success in the US, Hammer et al.[34] advance various theories to explain the relative ineffectiveness of worker directors in the US.

The impact of worker directors on board behaviour can, Hammer et al. argue, be usefully analysed using internal group representation and cooptation models of employee participation. According to interest group representation theory, worker directors are elected by constituencies who expect them to vocalise their concerns, including the pay determination of board members. Effective representation from the interest group constituency point of view demands a militant posture by the worker director. However, such a posture by the worker director is likely to cause other members of the board to caucus in a manner likely to exclude the worker director from exercising a significant input into strategic decision-making at board level. Thus, behaviour that is judged effective under an interest group representation constituency perspective may in fact be ineffective from the point of view of overall impact on the board.

Another view of worker director experiments, based upon resource dependency theory, is to look at board membership as a mechanism to produce a quiescent labour voice in decision-making. In order to achieve this, the worker director is coopted on to the board by the ruling elite of the organisation, and through a subtle process of socialisation into board practices (through an emphasis on fiduciary loyalty to the board) the worker director is disconnected from his/her constituency interests (at least from the interest group participation perspective).

The worker director becomes (under each of these scenarios) highly stressed and, caught in a web of conflicting roles, finds him/herself neutralised and ineffective. On both theoretical scenarios, therefore, the notion of employment involvement at board level appears to be problematic. How can effectiveness be increased given these grim scenarios?

The level of co-determination might be set below board level, with a joint council setup consisting of representatives of management and unions.[35] According to Parkinson, this council would be 'separate from the company's own decision-making structure' and 'employee representatives on such a body would have an extensive right to management information, a general right to be consulted in relation to matters affecting the workforce, and a right of co-determination in certain specified areas'.[36] A further route to employee representation is through the introduction of employee share ownership plans, which do not place employees at the decision-making forum but do allow employees, should they gain enough of the firm's shares, to exercise some control over the organisation. However, employee influence on the board is negligible under such schemes.

Empirical evidence for the introduction and impact of these initiatives is slight and, irrespective of the relative merits of such schemes, UK management is unlikely to introduce any measures which will hamper their ability to determine the organisation's direction and structure under increasingly competitive conditions. Given the decline in union membership and influence, the prospects for union voice at the decision-making table appear to be limited.

Where worker directors are involved, a number of initiatives may create more effective participation at board level. Such initiatives include increasing the provision of training in board procedures, financial management, and negotiation. Additionally, a further method to reduce the stress felt by worker directors under the interest group representation model would be to structure the expectations of constituents carefully to ensure that they realistically understand what the worker director can and cannot deliver. Finally, as with all board issues and structural mechanisms, it is the way in which the board process is enacted that is crucial.

CONCLUSION

This chapter has sought to defend the idea that trade unions can act as a useful agency mechanism with respect to the actions of employers. The negative aspects of union activity have been well aired and many of the arguments concerning monopoly power (which we have looked at briefly here), including coercion, featherbedding and shirking, are very familiar. In this chapter we have chosen to take a less familiar theme; the dangers inherent in companies where there is no union representation. If viewed as an example of an agency relationship, the union acts as agent of the employees with regard to the principal, the management, in order to constrain and monitor the performance of management in terms of the contract between the two parties. Without the presence of a union, there is a lack of a collective voice with which to pursue grievances and to negotiate better terms and conditions.

Developments such as HRM have emphasised the link between the individual and the organisation and have offered individual contracts at the expense of collective bargaining. But as we have touched upon, HRM can be viewed as a means of increasing managerial control while reducing worker autonomy and the quality of working life. Increased stress, greater surveillance, intolerance of mistakes and blame cultures, have all been identified as consequences of HRM systems, particularly when aligned to quality initiatives.

The weakness or absence of unions has also encouraged some

companies to hire and fire as they please, leading to downsizing programmes which, in a number of instances, were pursued too vigorously, resulting in local labour shortages.[37]

We have seen that unions provide useful benefits to their members, most importantly that of voice. But union membership and density are falling. The challenge to trade unions is therefore how to arrest the decline in support while continuing to play an influential role alongside the new management techniques within organisations.

ACKNOWLEDGEMENTS

We wish to thank John Kelly at LSE, and Diana Robertson at LBS, for helpful comments on an earlier draft of this chapter. The research was carried out under the auspices of a European Human Capital and Mobility Fellowship at London Business School.

NOTES

1 De George, R. T. (1995) *Business Ethics* (4th edn), Englewood Cliffs, NJ: Prentice-Hall.
2 For example, see Donaldson, J. (1989) *Key Issues in Business Ethics*, London: Academic Press.
3 Ibid.
4 Freeman, R. B. and Medoff, J. L. (1984) *What do Unions Do?*, New York: Basic Books.
5 Guest, D. (1989) 'HRM: Trades Unions and Industrial Relations', in Storey, J. (ed.), *New Perspectives on Human Resource Management*, London: Routledge, pp. 110–41.
6 Milner, S. (1995) 'The Coverage of Collective Pay-Setting Institutions in Britain, 1895–1990', *British Journal of Industrial Relations*, 33(1), March, pp. 69–92.
7 Purcell, J. (1993) 'The End of Institutional Industrial Relations', *Political Quarterly*, 64, pp. 6–23.
8 Machin, S. (1995) 'Plant Closures and Unionisation in British Establishments', *British Journal of Industrial Relations*, 33(1), March, pp. 55–68.
9 Morris, T. (1995) 'Annual Review Article 1994', *British Journal of Industrial Relations*, 33(1), March, pp. 117–35.
10 De George, *Business Ethics*.
11 Faith, R. L. and Reid, J. D. Jr (1987) 'An Agency Theory of Unionism', *Journal of Economic Behaviour and Organisation*, 8, pp. 39–60.
12 Ibid.
13 Freeman and Medoff, *What Do Unions Do?*

14 Ibid.

15 Faith and Reid, 'An Agency Theory of Unionism'.

16 Millward, N. (1994) *The New Industrial Relations?*, London: Policy Studies Institute.

17 Guest, 'HRM: Trades Unions and Industrial Relations'; see also Morris, 'Annual Review Article 1994'.

18 Norman, D. (1993) 'Trade Unions and New Management Techniques', in Crouch, C. and Marquand, D. (eds), *Ethics and Markets: Co-operation and Competition within Capitalist Economies*, Oxford: Basil Blackwell, pp. 111–25.

19 Storey, J. (1992) *Developments in the Management of Human Resources*, London: Routledge.

20 Norman, 'Trade Unions and New Management Techniques'.

21 Gregg, P. and Yates, A. (1991) 'Changes in Wage Settling Arrangements and Trade Union Presence in the 1980s', *British Journal of Industrial Relations*, 29(3), September, pp. 361–76.

22 Legge, K. (1989) 'HRM: A Critical Analysis', in Storey, *New Perspectives on Human Resource Management*, pp. 19–40.

23 Guest, 'HRM: Trades Unions and Industrial Relations'.

24 For example, see Storey, *Developments in the Management of Human Resources*.

25 Guest, 'HRM: Trades Unions and Industrial Relations', p. 55.

26 Morris, 'Annual Review Article 1994'.

27 Kelly, J. (1995) 'Review of *Employee Representation: Alternatives and Future Directions*, Kaufman, B. and Kleiner, M. (eds)', in *British Journal of Industrial Relations*, 33(1), March, pp. 149–50.

28 Delbridge, R. and Turnbull, P. (1992) 'The Management of Labour under Just-in-Time Systems', in Blyton, P. and Turnbull, P. (eds), *Reassessing Human Resource Management*, London: Sage, pp. 56–73.

29 Ibid., p. 60.

30 Kelly, 'Review of *Employee Representation: Alternatives and Future Directions*'.

31 Morris, 'Annual Review Article 1994'.

32 Parkinson, J. E. (1994) *Corporate Power and Responsibility: Issues in the Theory of Company Law*, Oxford: Clarendon Press, p. 408.

33 Ibid.

34 Hammer, W., Currall, S. C. and Stern, R. N. (1991) 'Worker Participation on Boards of Directors: A Study of Competing Roles', *Industrial and Labour Relations Review*, 44(4), July, pp. 661–80.

35 McCarthy, W. (1988) *The Future of Industrial Democracy*, London: Fabian Trust, No. 526.

36 Parkinson, *Corporate Power and Responsibility*, p. 421.

37 Ibid.

SELECT ANNOTATED
BIBLIOGRAPHY FOR
FURTHER READING

1 BUSINESS PHILOSOPHY: SEARCHING FOR AN AUTHENTIC ROLE

Allinson, Robert E. (1993) *Global Disasters: (Inquiries into Management Ethics)*, London: Prentice-Hall.

A key basis of Allinson's book is the claim that 'all global disasters are functions of mismanagement or a reflection of dysfunctional management' which come about 'as a result of thinking about things in the wrong way' (p. 6). He therefore focuses on the *process* of (good/bad) management decision-making and believes that all disasters are in principle preventable by designing a better humanistic organisation, thereby refuting those who believe that the complexity of technological systems *inevitably* leads to some disasters. Allinson relates these ideas to Japanese management and to TQM (total quality management). He then explores his theory through four highly interesting 'disaster' case-studies (the *Challenger* Space Shuttle explosion, the Kings Cross fire, the sinking of the *Herald of Free Enterprise*, and the Mount Erebus plane crash). Further references are also made to *EXXON Valdez*, Pan Am Flight 103, Chernobyl and Three Mile Island. He concludes that, in the face of complex techno-organisations, moral responsibility *is* still possible with better communication, a culture of TQM and safety, and an understanding of management 'professionalism' which includes taking an oath (similar to the doctor's Hippocratic oath). The value of Allinson's book is that he puts ethics inescapably at the feet of managers, but in *their* kind of language.

Pratley, Peter (1995) *The Essence of Business Ethics*, Hemel Hempstead, Herts: Prentice Hall International.

Perhaps a more apt title for this book would be 'The Essence of Business Ethics *Theory*' and it should be read in this light. The style of writing is somewhat laborious, but the ground it covers is both important and valuable. The stated scope of the book is 'to present useful ethical theories to business practitioners, and to improve the skills of reflective managers both in analyzing concrete moral issues and in deliberating and deciding upon stratagems for solving moral dilemmas' (p. xiv). It thus covers a large range of categories and sub-categories of ethical theories and relates them with varying success to numerous practical cases and scenarios. It also takes the reader through arguments and counter-arguments of the finer nuances of ethical theories, in an attempt to develop the reader's ability to improve their skills in ethical reflection, the importance of which is the subject of the first chapter. The value of this book is in its comprehensive cover of ethical theory while demonstrating both the benefits and limitations of applying such theories to everyday practical business situations.

2 WHOSE BUSINESS IS IT ANYWAY? – THE QUESTION OF SUSTAINABILITY

Hawken, Paul (1993) *The Ecology of Commerce: (How business can save the planet)*, London: Weidenfeld & Nicolson.

Paul Hawken is one of America's leading green entrepreneurs, having co-founded two substantial businesses. He therefore has some reason to be listened to in relation to the title of his book. Taking a systems approach he argues that business and commerce of the future should be understood more like a biological system – self-sustaining, non-wasteful and self-regenerating. Business has the power to reverse ecological destruction (an ethical imperative), and he suggests ways in which the world of work can be redesigned for inbuilt sustainability. The book is also a call to business and government leaders to adopt a cooperative programme which, he maintains, will bring prosperity and employment, as well as rescuing the ecology. The book is well-referenced and reads well, using numerous examples with insightful comments. His diagnosis is very persuasive and his prognosis makes much sense. But, like many such 'save the world' books, the solution's enactment depends on powerful business and government leaders adopting the new paradigm; history suggests this will be a long process unless some really severe ecological crisis speeds up the adoption of new attitudes at all levels. Nevertheless, this is one of the best books of its genre in recent times.

Petrella, Ricardo (1995) *Limits to Competition: Towards a New Social Contract*, Cambridge, Mass: MIT Press.

This book is reminiscent of, and in a way a follow-up to, *Limits to Growth* of the Club of Rome. It is a critique on the globalisation ('Triadisation' – chapter 2) of business and trade. It was written by eighteen intellectuals and researchers from Europe, North America and Japan, under the direction of Ricardo Petrella, member of the EU's Social Research Division. The answer to the question 'can competition continue to rule the planet?' (chapter 3) is an emphatic *no*. The current global business practice, driven along by the aggressive winner–loser ethos of competitiveness, does not make any economic, ecological, social or ultimately any ethical sense. The dominant competition-cum-business paradigm has come increasingly under scrutiny by those who articulate, as it were, 'views from the top'. The Club of Rome and the International Council for Sustainable Development (ICSD), for example, are perceived to belong to the 'new enlightened elites', those at the cutting edge of moral, cultural and human rights issues. The 'new global civic society' (chapter 1), however, also has its representatives at grassroots, at the level of 'developing planetary consciousness'. There are at the moment approximately 450,000 interest groups and non-government organisations throughout the world, a large proportion of whom have a globalist and planetary outlook. They represent 600 to 800 million members, with 5 to 6 million leaders. Coming in the wake of 'Limits to Growth', *Limits to Competition* challenges the most persistent and potentially destructive myth since the industrial revolution, namely that our salvation resides in competitive 'well-having', rather than in participatory 'well-being'. The book has already been hailed as 'revolutionary' and 'an introduction to the 21st century'. It is well worth a look.

3 CORPORATE GOVERNANCE AND ETHICS

Prentice, D. D. and Holland, P. R. J. (eds) (1993) *Contemporary Issues in Corporate Governance*, Oxford: Clarendon Press.

This book is an edited collection of papers from the second Oxford Law Colloquium on corporate governance. A distinguished panel of contributors, including Sir Adrian Cadbury, Martin Lipton, Eddy Wymeersch, Paul Rutteman and D. D. Prentice among others, examine corporate governance on a national and comparative level. The papers are arranged under broad themes concerning the role of financial disclosure, institutional shareholders, takeover bids and litigation in improving corporate governance, and each chapter contains a wealth of implicit and explicit concerns for ethical practice.

Parkinson, J. E. (1995) *Corporate Power and Responsibility: Issues in the Theory of Company Law*, Oxford: Oxford University Press.

This comprehensive work has as its broad theme the notion that corporate power should not be guided purely with a view to profit maximisation, but that it should be exercised in the public interest. For this to be achieved, corporate decision-making has to be made more responsive to the social environment. Parkinson provides sophisticated critiques of current corporate governance arrangements, stakeholder theory and transaction cost economics, and examines the way company law might be changed to ensure corporations pursue social policy objectives.

The Report of the Committee on the Financial Aspects of Corporate Governance (The Cadbury Report), London: Gee & Co, 1992.

The Cadbury Committee was set up by the accountancy professions and the London Stock Exchange in the wake of a series of high profile cases of corporate fraud and failure. Cadbury's remit was to establish a code of best practice for the financial aspects of corporate governance, and its proposals are now widely accepted by UK public companies. The main recommendations – splitting the roles of chairman and chief executive, the presence of independent non-executive directors on the board, mandatory audit and remuneration committees – have sought to establish stronger checks and balances to executive power, though critics have said that the code stifles the entrepreneurial spirit of top management and, moreover, the recommendations would do little to stop a rogue CEO (such as Maxwell).

4 BUSINESS AND ITS SOCIAL RESPONSIBILITY

Cannon, Tom (1994) *Corporate Responsibility: A Textbook on Business Ethics, Governance, Environment: Roles and Responsibilities*, London: Pitman.

This book traces modern-day notions of corporate responsibility back to the Industrial Revolution in a review that takes in the responsibilities of business, governance and compliance, the environment, and the challenges posed by the economically and socially disadvantaged. It strikes a happy balance between a sound theoretical understanding of the issues and a practical guide to action in this area, drawing on a wide variety of national and international case studies. The book provides a valuable guide to the opportunities and threats facing business today in its ever-changing relationship with the rest of society.

Jennings, Marie (ed.) (1990) *Guide to Corporate Citizenship*, London: Director Books.

The premise that this book seeks to explore is that ethics and profits are entirely compatible. The book argues that today's organisations need to develop new approaches to corporate responsibility and to adopt new management techniques in the face of these responsibilities. It offers practical advice – from a range of business practitioners – on a company's relationship with several of its key 'stakeholder' groups, including employees, customers and shareholders. Useful appendices feature case studies in corporate citizenship, codes of ethics, and further sources of help and advice.

School for Advanced Urban Studies (SAUS) (ed.) (1993) *Good Business? Case Studies in Corporate Social Responsibility*, Bristol: SAUS Publications with New Consumer.

This collection of short papers offers an illuminating introduction to many aspects of implementing socially responsible business practices. The case studies include: British Airways' approach to the environment; the Cooperative Bank's ethical policy; and B&Q's employment of older workers. Each concise study examines both the successes of the programme and the problems encountered in developing and implementing the initiatives. The book is a useful source for those seeking to gain an insight into the

range of measures organisations are adopting in an effort to put into practice 'good business' principles.

5 THE BUSINESS ORGANISATION: A LOCUS FOR MEANING AND MORAL GUIDANCE

Frederick, William C., Post, James. E. and Davis, Keith (1992) *Business and Society*, (7th edn), New York: McGraw-Hill.

This is a comprehensive textbook covering four major areas of the subject, together with ten international case-studies. Part One, the corporation in society, sets out the stakeholder model and reviews the social responsibility of the corporation, ethical dilemmas in business, and the hallmarks of a socially responsible management. The constraints of working in a global context are discussed in Part Two, with special reference to the multi-national corporation. Part Three then goes on to explore public policy issues, especially business's relations with government. Part Four is devoted to ways of responding to corporate stakeholders, including men, women and the family.

Angular, Francis J. (1994) *Managing Corporate Ethics*, New York: Oxford University Press.

This book is about the relationship of business performance, corporate val-ues and ethics. It draws on numerous cases to show how important the sub-ject is for business success. The availability of effective means of introducing to the corporation a consistent value system is described in detail. There are numerous tables and charts illustrating the process of maintaining corporate excellence, which is based on a policy of moral integrity in all corporate operations.

6 THE PSYCHOLOGICAL CONTRACT: ENACTING ETHICO-POWER

Handy, Charles (1994), *The Empty Raincoat*, London: Hutchinson.

It is Handy's reworking of the 'Federalist Idea', and in particular the notions of 'twin citizenship' and 'subsidiarity', which are of interest here. The former, which he defines in terms of 'a local belonging and a broader, bigger citizenship, both in our organisation and in society', finds a parallel in the idea of the *contextualised autonomy* which defines the individual and is developed in the paper. The latter, the notion of 'subsidiarity', suggests that power belongs to the lowest possible point of the organisation. Handy construes 'subsidiarity' as 'reverse delegation' – the delegation of the parts to the centre. This crucial ingredient of federalism is also important for the release of ethico-power.

Reed, Michael (1992) *The Sociology of Organisations: Themes, Perspectives and Prospects*, Hemel Hempstead, Herts: Harvester Wheatsheaf.

Reed provides an excellent overview of the analytical frameworks, theory groups and current issues in organisational analysis. Several of the features which he suggests are indicative of the post-structuralist theory group; notions such as the critique of bureaucratic rationality in favour of multiple rationalities or contextual rationality, the importance of trust relations, the critique of utilitarianism and the existence of multiple organisational realities, are mirrored in the discussion on ethico-power.

Wheatley, Margaret J. (1994) *Leadership and the New Science*, San Francisco: Berrett-Koehler Publishers.

This book is particularly helpful for its presentation, in an informed and accessible way, of the notion of *autopoiesis*. This idea, entailing as it does a process of self-organisation, frees employees from strict rules and controls and suggests more time should be spent facilitating strong relationships among people. Drawing for her inspiration on chaos theory and quantum mechanics, Wheatley argues that a system (and especially an organisation) is defined by the relationships and fields that bind the parts together to make a whole. An ethics of organisational life requires strong bonding mechanisms, such as trust, value coordination and the sharing of information. These elements are addressed in this book and their relationship to organisational leadership is explored.

Gambetta, Diego (ed.) (1988) *Trust: Making and Breaking Co-operative Relations*, Oxford: Basil Blackwell.

Diego Gambetta edits an interdisciplinary book with contributions from the field of philosophy, social psychology, economics, political theory, sociology, history, social anthropology and ethology. While all the papers are of interest, David Good's contribution is of special interest for the notion of the *psychological contract*, and has been cited in this chapter. Perhaps the most important facet of his argument, at least for our purposes, is the attention he gives to discovering the 'conditions under which individuals are willing to trust one another in novel circumstances'. In the chaotic environment of organisational change, such a discovery would aid the development of an ethical organisational culture.

7 ACTING PROFESSIONALLY: SOMETHING THAT BUSINESS ORGANISATIONS AND INDIVIDUALS BOTH DESIRE?

Chadwick, Ruth (ed.) (1994) *Ethics and the Professions*, Aldershot: Avebury Press.

This book comprises the formal conference proceedings of the 1991 Conference held in Manchester by the Society for Applied Philosophy. Including contributions from a variety of European countries and from a range of disciplines, it provides an interesting insight into what it means to be a professional – from an engineer to a social worker. While the points of view represented are very different, if taken as a whole – particularly with the excellent introduction by Chadwick – the book provides the basis from which philosophical frameworks can be construed as to what ethics might mean in relation to different professions, including the profession of moral philosophy itself. The view of professions that emerges is a strictly moral one and, therefore, one which is traditional, rather than the much wider definition that equates 'professional' with well-educated, of high status, and so on. The narrower view emerging from this volume looks for special client–professional relationships in which there is present a notion of altruism and a particular good.

Henry, Chris (ed.) (1994) *Professional Ethics and Organisational Change*, London: Edward Arnold.

Henry's book looks at how ethics can be used as a managerial tool to assist in easing the transition from one state of being to another in the context of organisational bureaucracy. Arguably, the book is more about the psychology of change than the philosophical construction of a moral community, though there is an interdependency in these two phenomena which should not be overlooked. Focusing on the research carried out at the University of Central Lancashire in 1992 on its own ethics and values, the book examines how doing an ethics audit can both affect and reflect on the culture of an organisation. Predominantly concerned with a Higher Education institution, the book emphasises the transferability of the process to other organisations, not least the National Health Service. The process is particularly helpful during periods of change, as is exemplified by the introduction of NHS Trusts and the conversion from polytechnics into universities in the education sector. Different chapters identify the interests of various stakeholders in an organisation. The quite diverse points of view contained in the book are wrought into a more or less cohesive volume by editorial linking passages between each section and chapter. The book is illustrated by the most delightful cartoons. The artist depicts the abstract philosophical concepts as 'snapshot' practical situations. This feature underlines the overall aim of the book to be of practical use in professional settings. Generally, the book is an interesting pot-pourri of the roles ethics can play in working life.

Koehn, Daryl (1994) *The Ground of Professional Ethics*, London: Routledge.

This well-written and conceptually well-designed book presents a picture of professionals that will regenerate one's faith in the reality of professional ethics. It describes clearly and compassionately the moral relationship that exists between professional and client. It understands 'professional' as the moral term, and discusses the various constructions of essential and intrinsic 'good' in professional intention. Less cynical about professionalism than many recent analyses, the book brings into the foreground an aspect of passion into the personal commitment of many professionals to the well-being of their clients.

Callahan, J. C. (ed.) (1988) *Ethical Issues in Professional Life*, New York: Oxford University Press.

A useful collection of essays, this book gives a comprehensive view of what professional ethics is taken to be, together with detailed coverage of recurring problems from confidentiality to deception. The volume also looks at the relationship the professions have to society at large, rather than just to individual clients, and deals with some cases where there may be moral conflict arising out of these respective positions.

8 CODES OF ETHICS: SOME USES AND ABUSES

Anthony, Peter D. (1986) *The Foundation of Management*, London: Tavistock Publications.

Anthony's book provides a well-written account of management and its role in the modern business world. What distinguishes this work as an excellent piece of scholarship is its reconstruction of a moral history of management in Britain and an in-depth explanation of its gradual rise to power. The final chapters are particularly interesting, where Anthony attempts to outline a moral foundation for management with reference to the excellent work of the philosopher and critic, Alasdair MacIntyre.

Argyris, Chris (1990) *Overcoming Organizational Defenses: facilitating organizational learning*, Boston, Mass.: Ally & Bacon.

Argyris's book is at the cutting edge of organisation theory, examining the ways in which organisations learn. The main focus of the book revolves around the idea of 'organisational defensive routines', which impede communication within an organisation and can prevent crucial issues from ever seeing the light of day. In response to these knotty problems he develops the idea of 'double loop learning', which has a clear moral dimension to it.

Jackall, Robert (1988) *Moral Mazes: The World of Corporate Managers*, New York: Oxford University Press.

Moral Mazes provides a stimulating, if somewhat disquieting account of life in the modern corporate world. It draws on the experiences of a large number of corporate managers and business persons and subjects these to an analysis which is both rigorous and entertaining. The picture he paints is rich in the detail of everyday life, which shows just how difficult it is to escape its moral mazes.

Winkler, Earl R. and Coombs, Jerrold R. (eds) (1993) *Applied Ethics: A Reader*, Oxford: Basil Blackwell.

This Reader is a rich source of material on the contemporary debates within applied ethics, including environmentalism, biomedical ethics, and business ethics. There are also some valuable chapters on the methodology of applied ethics at the beginning of the book, which cannot fail to be of interest to those of us who are currently engaged in business ethics research. One of the most remarkable aspects of this reader is that it shows how similar debates are arising in quite different areas of applied ethics.

9 WHISTLEBLOWING AND ITS ALTERNATIVES

Hunt, Geoffrey (ed.) (1994) *Whistleblowing in the Health Service: Accountability, Law and Professional Practice*, London: Edward Arnold.

This book focuses on the issues and effects that arise from whistleblowing in the healthcare environment. The UK experience is compared with that of the USA, and the core issues of accountability and legal rights from the managerial, clinical and public perspectives are explored in detail. The legal implications of confidentiality and 'gagging' are considered, and suggestions are made as to how accountability can be reformed. The question of self-regulation through employee vigilance is discussed, and accounts are given by whistleblowers of their experiences. Although obviously aimed at the healthcare environment, this book has much wider relevance because of the commonalities in most *organisational* contexts, as well as the increasing conflicts of interest due to the movement towards *professionalising* many jobs.

Vinten, Gerald (ed.) (1995) *Whistleblowing: Subversion or Corporate Citizenship?* London: Paul Chapman Publishing.

The aim of Vinten's book is to provide a balanced approach to whistleblowing – defined as informing on illegal and unethical practices in the workplace. Contributors include academics, lawyers, and whistleblowers describing their own experiences. The book considers the US and UK legal background (in the USA some statutory protection of whistleblowers exists), along with professional perspectives on whistleblowing. The author considers how to use whistleblowers positively, and a possible Code of Practice, agreed procedures and preventative measures are put forward to protect both whistleblower and employer.

Winfield, Marlene (1990) *Minding your own business: self-regulation and whistleblowing in British companies*, London: Social Audit.

This book studies how British companies regulate themselves, and recommends more effective strategies for the future. Among the issues considered are: how companies might develop ethical cultures; why and how to make employees into self-regulators; the possible roles for trade unions and professional associations in ethical policy-making; and examples of more and less effective policy documents. Accounts of the experiences of whistleblowers are provided to illustrate the key issues. The recommendation is for a strategy, not of more rigid external controls, but of self-regulation based on an employee's value to the business, and their needs and problems. In this context, whistleblowers are viewed as a 'meritorious' safety net to be protected.

Two important support organisations for whistleblowers in the UK are:

PUBLIC CONCERN AT WORK   PCAW was set up to promote good practice and compliance with the law in the public, private and voluntary sectors. It is a charity which has been designated a legal advice centre by the Bar Council, and offers free legal advice and assistance to employees who are concerned about serious malpractice in the workplace, but are unsure what to do, or who fear that they may be victimised if they raise their concerns internally. PCAW's address is: Public Concern At Work, Lincoln's Inn House, 42 Kingsway, London WC2B 6EN; Tel: 0171 404 6609; Fax: 0171 404 6576.

FREEDOM TO CARE   Freedom to Care aims to support conscientious employees in the public services who speak out in the public interest. They campaign for the legal, administrative and managerial reforms necessary to encourage freedom of speech in the workplace. Regular meetings are held, a thrice yearly newsletter is published, and members are kept up to date with all important developments in this area. Their address is: Membership Secretary, Freedom To Care, PO Box 125, West Molesey, Surrey, KT8 1YE.

10 BUSINESS ETHICS AND THE ACTIVITIES OF MULTINATIONALS

De George, Richard T. (1993) *Competing with Integrity in International Business*, New York: Oxford University Press.

De George examines the moral debates that inevitably arise when doing business in an international setting. With the objective of aiding companies to compete with integrity, De George provides guidelines for those doing business in less developed countries and for those dealing with dangerous technologies. Strategies are also presented for how to compete in a corrupt environment.

Donaldson, Thomas (1989) *The Ethics of International Business*, New York: Oxford University Press.

Donaldson address international business ethics by reviewing the following topics: the moral foundations of multinationals; the notion of a fundamental international right; and an ethical algorithm to determine whether certain business practices should transcend national and cultural borders. The concepts are tied together using in-depth case studies, such as Union Carbide subjecting Bhopal citizens to higher technological risks.

An important organisation concerning Multi-National Ethics is: Transparency International (TI), (The coalition against corruption in international business transactions), Heylstrasse 33, D-10825 Berlin, Germany. *Tel:* (49)-30-787-59-08, *Fax:* (49)-30-787-57-07, *E'mail:* ti@contrib.de, *Internet:* http://www.is.in-berlin.de/Service/ti.html

11 BUSINESS ETHICS AND THE CHANGING GENDER BALANCE

Gilligan, C. (1982) *In a Different Voice: Psychological Theory and Women's Development*, 2nd edn 1993, Boston: Harvard University Press.

In her 'Letter to Readers', added for the thirty-second printing of her book in 1993, Gilligan reflects on the three kinds of questions most frequently raised by her 1982 text: the question of difference; the question of female and male development; and the question of 'voice'. One of Gilligan's most important contributions to the debate on differences between women and men was to point to its socially and politically constructed nature, showing how female development was judged deviant by male scholars. In asking questions about the *interpretation* of difference, Gilligan thus challenged male dominance of language and culture from within the conventional discourse of psychology. What shines through, as you read the book, is Gilligan's concern to listen to women and hear their voices proclaim the interconnectedness of human life against the male tendency to objectify human relationships into abstract principles and rules. Gilligan's discussion of Amy and Jake, used to illustrate her case for a female ethic of care and male logic of justice, can be found in chapter 2 of *In a Different Voice*.

Those interested in the development and use of her work are referred to Gilligan, C. (1988) *Mapping the Moral Domain*, Harvard University Press, a book of readings. The contribution by Jack and Jack on women lawyers is particularly recommended.

Davidson, M. J. and Cooper, C. L. (1992) *Shattering the Glass Ceiling: The Woman Manager*, London: Paul Chapman Publishing.

Cary Cooper is one of the foremost authorities on stress at work, having researched and published prodigiously on the subject. He has also published previously with Marilyn Davidson on the subject of Stress and Women Managers in a 1982 text, *High Pressure: Working Lives of Women Managers*, published by Fontana. Although the authors tend to adopt a social psychological perspective (despite arguing for a multi-disciplinary approach)[1] and focus their attention on stress at work, the book does offer a number of interesting insights into women and management. The first chapter provides a good overview of women in business and management in the 1990s, documents the changing patterns of women's work, outlines the position of women holding high office in management, public bodies and politics, and discusses issues for the future, adopting an optimistic stance. The chapters which follow outline the problems faced by women at work and include discussion on stress, skill, personality, role theory, work relationships, careers and the interplay between home and work.

The final chapter is entitled *Positive approaches to helping women into management*, where the authors consider such matters as flexible work patterns, career work and child care schemes, corporate policy on equal opportunities, assertiveness, trade unions and the role of the law.

Humm, M. (ed.) (1992) *Feminism: A Reader*, Hemel Hempstead, Herts: Harvester Wheatsheaf.

Maggie Humm has published widely on feminism. Her works include the 1989 text *The Dictionary of Feminist Theory*. Humm opens the book with a 'chronology of events and texts from 1900 to the present'. Her headings, 'Feminist Politics' and 'Feminist Writing', are helpful in defining feminism historically as both theoretical and practical – a 'social force' as she calls it. Feminism, she suggests, 'probably dates from the seventeenth century' and can 'stand for a belief in sexual equality combined with a commitment to eradicate sexist domination and to transform society'. The history of feminism, in Britain and America, is dealt with in chapter 1 of the book.

The rest of the book introduces a variety of readings organised around a number of selected themes and perspectives. These include first and second wave feminism, difference, psychoanalysis, nature, sexuality and reproduction, peace, philosophy, history, culture, language and writing, education, and the following perspectives: Socialist/Marxist, Asian, Black and Women of Colour, Lesbian and Liberal. The chapters are introduced, and each reading is prefaced by a commentary on the author whose work follows. Although the readings (and introductions) are painfully short, and although there are some gaps in the coverage which Humm herself acknowledges (e.g. ecofeminism and theology), this Reader nonetheless provides a sound introduction to feminist scholarship and will whet the appetite to seek out those interesting original sources!

Business Ethics: A European Review, (1993), 2(1), January, Oxford: Blackwell.

This journal, edited by Jack Mahoney (Dixons Professor of Business Ethics and Social Responsibility at London Business School), carried a special focus on *Women in Business* in the January 1993 issue, and it includes a number of interesting articles on the subject.

Useful UK addresses

Equal Opportunities Commission, Overseas House. Quay Street, Manchester M3 3HN, Tel: 0161 833 9244.
The Feminist Library, 5 Westminster Bridge Road, London SE1 7XJ, Tel: 0171 928 7789.

12 PRIVATISED ETHICS: THE CASE OF THE REGULATED UTILITIES

Goyder, George (1993) *The Responsible Company: A Blueprint for the Responsible Company*, London: Adamantine Press.

Goyder has long been a proponent of the notion of *industrial democracy*, and not only does he have a publishing record over 45 years long, but has also had a distinguished career in business. He sees no essential conflict between industrial and social purposes – private sector companies are key mediating institutions in a democracy, and their role is to make economic and social-welfare values compatible. Corporate power brings responsibility for justice and fulfilment in the lives of stakeholders. He argues that corporate law is inhibited by outmoded company law and regulation, the dominance of shareholder owners over employees and customers, a lack of collective purpose, and the absence of holistic management. He then argues for some key reforms: a restyling of the notion of 'general purposes' in company law; the periodic redemption of equity capital; directors to be trustees; employees to be shareholders; a new-style AGM; and a social audit. In keeping the question of 'ownership' alive, Goyder brings an important element to the business ethics debate.

Foster, C. D. (1992) *Privatisation, Public Ownership and the Regulation of Natural Monopoly*, Oxford: Basil Blackwell.

Foster provides a comprehensive overview of the regulation of natural monopoly 'network' industries, and of the social and ethical framework in which they are managed. His strong historical perspective includes the nineteenth century railway network, the period of nationalisation, the reaction towards privatisation, and independent 'incentive' regulation after 1979. Price and quality-of-service controls are distinguished from profit control, and UK and US practices are contrasted. Key questions in ethics and accountability are reviewed, including: can independence be preserved?

13 TRADE UNIONS AND ETHICS: UNIONS AS AGENTS

Norman, D. (1993) 'Trade Unions and New Management Techniques', in Crouch, C. and Marquand, D., *Ethics and Markets: Co-operation and Competition within Capitalist Economics*, Oxford: Blackwell, pp. 111–25.

Norman argues that the challenges posed to trade unions by the adoption of new management techniques are neither particularly novel nor particularly threatening to trade unions, when compared to those challenges posed to union density by industrial restructuring away from union heartlands and towards the service sector, where trade unions domains have been traditionally weak. Nonetheless, the introduction of novel HRM techniques (such as teamworking, flexibility, and the advent of 'personal contracts' replacing standardised collective bargaining agreements) has challenged trade unions to be responsive to managerial initiatives if they are to maintain an authoritative voice at workplace level.

The increase in the adoption of new managerial techniques such as Total Quality Management, with its emphasis on the creation of an error reduction culture rather than one of error avoidance has been prompted by the intensification of competition from newly industrialising countries with low labour costs, as well as the increasing strength of well established Pacific Rim competitors. Additionally, the privatisation wave has imported new managerial techniques to the 'sheltered' public sector. The intensification of competition, coupled with intense cost cutting, has eroded many trade-union-organised jobs. Utilising individualist HRM techniques such as personal contracts has further eroded trade union authority in industries such as telecommunications, particularly within managerial ranks.

Trade unions seem to have adopted a strategy of cooperating with many of the new management initiatives, fearful of further marginalisation and being cast in the role of 'Luddites' in the new industrial order. The new-found managerial ascendancy in newly privatised companies, the author argues, has, however, had the effect of creating divisions within large sectors of the workforce.

Freeman, R. B. and Medoff, James L. (1984) *What Do Unions Do?*, New York: Basic Books.

This classic work argues that trade unions have two 'faces': a monopoly face and a voice/response face. Proponents of the 'monopoly face' view of unions argue that unions have monopoly power which they use to raise wages above competitive levels, thus reducing the efficient functioning of the labour market and impairing economic growth. The proponents of the 'voice/response' view argue that trade unions have beneficial effects on economic growth through the creation of more equitable rules to govern the operation of the internal labour market. Using extensive data from the US, the author's empirical findings break down into three categories: efficiency; distribution of income; and social organisation. They show that the monopoly assertion that trade unions reduce employment in the unionised sector is justified. On the 'voice/response' side, trade unions create more equitable workplace practices and compensation packages which are more valuable to employees (including pension provision for groups who are likely to be exposed and otherwise uncovered). This is associated with greater productivity in many settings, particularly where the quality of the employee relations climate is good. On balance, the authors argue, unionism raises social efficiency.

In relation to distribution of income, the balance of evidence is in favour of the 'voice/response' face – trade unions lower labour turnover, allowing the accumulation of valuable skill within firms, reducing wage inequality, but also lowering profits which would normally go to higher income persons.

Social Organisation effects found suggest that undemocratic practices within unions are rare, and trade unions provide a valuable voice for all employees, particularly in the creation of enabling social legislation which creates a platform of minimum rights for workers.

NOTE

1 For a critique of social psychological discourse and a call for alternative perspectives, see Clark, H., Chandler, J. and Barry, J. (eds) (1994) *Organisation and Identities*, London: Chapman & Hall.

INDEX